Violence, Homelessness and Running

Rev. Dean C. Jones, PhD

Parson's Porch Books

Violence, Homelessness and Running
ISBN: Softcover 978-1-949888-58-4
Copyright © 2016 by Dean C. Jones

All rights reserved. No part of this book may be reproduced or transmitted in any form or by any means, electronic or mechanical, including photocopying, recording, or by any information storage and retrieval system, without permission in writing from the publisher.

Photography by Rennie Zapp

To order additional copies of this book, contact:

Parson's Porch Books
1-423-475-7308
www.parsonsporch.com

Parson's Porch Books is an imprint of Parson's Porch & Company (PP&C) in Cleveland, Tennessee. PP&C is an innovative non-profit organization which raises money by publishing books of noted authors, representing all genres. All donations from contributors and profits from publishing are shared with the poor.

Violence, Homelessness and Running

Introduction

The book; "Learning to Walk in the Dark," by New York Times bestselling author Barbara Brown Taylor 1 was one of the most insightful publications of 2014. In her book, Taylor paints a new picture of the "dark." As she documents, some of the most important spiritual happenings have occurred in the dark. My book is a trilogy of walking in the dark. I share stories from my work in the physical darkness as I walked the streets of different cities late at night, sometimes all night long.

In ministry at night in the "worst" part of the city it was not unusual to walk where the cloud of potential violence was part of the scene. This introduces another kind of darkness, that of the darkness of the spirit. Today we live with the stress of potential violence of another kind from the awareness of terrorist activity in different parts of our world.

Violence, whether written in the bold letters of mass murder or in the pain of personal, even self-directed violence as in suicide is always very difficult to walk into. Learning to walk with people in their own world of pain is not easy. I share my stories of outreach to people at night on the streets of five different cities.

Another form of darkness of the spirit is on display in most cities today in the form of homelessness. What is it like to be alone at night in the city? Walking with someone who is in this situation is not easy. It was not an easy thing for me to do.

It was not an easy task for me to recall the personal darkness which commanded most of the lives of people I helped at night. But I do not stop there in my book. There was the physical darkness of the night hours, then the darkness in the life of people. Finally, and even more difficult for me to handle, was the darkness in my own life. For the first time I share in the pages which follow my memories of a divorce after 45 years of marriage and the death of my second wife after only two years of marriage. I am blessed now in my third marriage.

In a book about ministry it might seem strange to introduce the topic of running. This is the first time I have shared stories of my running.

Some of this was done as a way to promote my work of night ministry. But I started running before I was involved in Operation Nightwatch. Now, some 40 years later, running and other kinds of physical exercise have become very popular.

A final comment is in order. I am now looking forward to my 84th birthday in a few months. Although we are now blessed with a growing number of people who live into their 80's or 90's this part of the population is sometimes not in the popular press. I can look back to my years as a child, born during the Great Depression and living through World War II. Whatever your age I welcome you in my walk and run through the days of my life.

Chapter 1
A Timely Story Begins in Seattle: A Book for Today

In this book I invite you to come along with me in my life journey. Perhaps a few comments are in order as we begin. I have always been involved in the Church. The specifics of this involvement have changed through the years as well as the church I have been involved in. In the long ago past I gave the sermon Sunday morning and Sunday evening. For many years now I have been sitting in the pew on Sunday. I attend every Sunday. It is hard for me to imagine a life without a sense of faith, of the ever-present reality of an eternal God and His Grace. I applaud President Obama for singing a few lines of the old hymn "Amazing Grace" at a recent eulogy.

As I reflect, I am impressed by the way a church service follows a carefully pre-planned program. The Sunday morning church bulletin is a guide through a time that has no unexpected moments. This is in keeping with the main function of the Church; to sustain a sense of solidarity, of deep inner peace in a world that can become uncertain, even dangerous. This is most dramatically illustrated by violence of any form.

We are now living in very different times, making this book very timely. Today violence and the threat of violence have become major news items. Violence can assume many different forms. This includes the self violence of alcoholism, drug addiction or suicide. As this is written it is not unusual for families to be shown pictures with the evening news which highlight some form of violence. These pictures have shown, for example, an ISIS man, dressed all in black with head and face covered as he stands with a knife in hand beside an American journalist in Syria who is dressed in an orange prison uniform with hands tied behind his back. This journalist and another were beheaded. On the eve of the 13th anniversary of the tragic attack of 9/11 President Barack Obama and members of congress were drafting a strategy to respond to the growing threat of ISIS in Iraq, Syria and elsewhere. The shadow of the tragedy which unfolded in New York and Washington D.C. on September 11, 2001 remains over our country. There were four coordinated attacks on 9/11, killing almost 3,000 people and causing over $10 billion in property and infrastructure damage. Most of this damage was suffered at the North and South Towers of the World Trade Center Buildings. Four passenger jets were hijacked in this terrorist attack.

On April 19, 1995, 168 people were killed and over 680 were injured in bombings in Oklahoma City. In 1999 two senior high school students at Columbine High School in Colorado murdered 12 fellow students plus a teacher and injured 21 others before taking their own lives. On April 16, 2007, a senior at Virginia Tech School killed 32 people and wounded 17 others before taking his own life. The darkness of a Century Movie Theatre in Aurora, Colorado was shattered on the evening of July 20, 2012 when James Holmes broke into the theatre, displaying an array of firearms. He proceeded to shoot into the audience, killing 12 people and injuring 70 others. On December of 2012 Adam Lanza, a 20-year-old, shot 20 children and adult staff members at Sandy Hook Elementary School in Newtown, Connecticut before shooting himself and his mother. The Church has never been immune from the tragedy of some form of violence. A recent example unfolded in Charleston, South Carolina on the evening of June 17, 2015 when a 21-year-old White man walked through the welcoming doors of a well-known, historic, African Methodist Episcopal (AME) Church to join a small Wednesday evening Bible-Prayer service. He sat with nine church members for an hour before pulling a gun and going on a shooting spree. Nine church members were killed, including the pastor of the Church.

On the morning of Thursday, October 1, 2015, Chris Harper Mercer, a 26-year-old man, opened fire in a classroom at Umpqua Community College in Roseburg, Oregon. Nine people were killed and seven wounded. Mr. Mercer then shot and killed himself after a shootout with police. One of the unique features of this mass killing was that the gunman asked people to stand up and identify their religious preference before he began shooting. He specifically targeted those who said that they were Christian.

Major scenes of violence have now become the hallmark of our time. The entire world stood in shock after the bold attack in the middle of Paris on the evening of November 13, 2015. Suicide bombers and men armed with serious weapons of murder killed 130 people and injured many more. ISIS was proud to take responsibility for this scene of massive tragedy.

And the bullets keep flying. On December 2, 2015 two people, faces covered with dark masks and carrying several weapons, walked into a large room at the Inland Regional Center, home for outreach services in San Bernardino, California. In a shooting rampage 14 people were killed and 21 were injured. The shooters were husband and wife, Syed Farook and Tashfeen Malik. They were subsequently killed in a shoot-out with law enforcement officers. A six-month old baby was left without parents as another tragic result of this event. There were signs that this couple had some connection to ISIS. On Sunday evening, December 6 President Obama, speaking to the nation from the Oval Office, said that this couple had walked down the "dark path of radicalization," labeling the incident as "an act of terrorism."

The community of faith has always had a powerful role in the prevention of and responses to violence of any form. I have never been personally involved in any form of mass violence. But newspaper headlines and full-color pictures on TV are now prompting more attention to all forms of violence. In my work of night ministry, I walked the downtown streets of different cities in places of the city known for violence. This took the form of drive-by shootings, open use of illegal drugs, suicide and alcohol or drug addiction. Today it is important to hear from anyone who has walked where events are unpredictable and violence is an ever-present possibility.

On Sunday the prayers of the people usually include mention of those who are "homeless, poor, sick or disabled." Homelessness is a stark reality in many cities across our country today. This again makes this book very timely since my work at night always included people who were homeless. In 2014 at least 20 people died, alone and homeless in the progressive college town of Boulder, Colorado.

In March of 2015 the L.A. Times reported that Los Angeles County hosted some 58,000 homeless people. On Sunday, June 14, 2015, Joe Mozingo, a reporter with the L.A. Times, offered a timely article with compelling pictures of the present situation in the city of San Bernardino, California. In this city formerly "middle class" housing and neighborhoods have now been replaced by people struggling to survive. In July of 2015 MSNBC ran a special series titled "Geography of Poverty" (in America). San Francisco has now become a destination for high-tech companies. Housing has become very expensive, adding to the number who have no place to live. A man, homeless in this city for six months was seen recently holding up a hand-printed message on a discarded piece of cardboard for all to see as he stood on a street corner in the Mission District. His tear-stained message was simple:

Miserable, Hungry and Completely Without Any Shred of Hope

My 20 years of full-time work in night ministry included many contacts with people who lived on the street. This gives me the opportunity to share stories which give a better understanding of the term "homeless."

At the polar opposite from violence or homelessness, today various forms of physical fitness are also getting a lot of attention. Over 40 years ago a local policeman stopped me as I was running along the shoulder of a road in Indiana. The sight of someone running was very unusual. I assume that he thought that I was running from a theft or some other illegal activity. Now running and cycling are familiar sights. Most cities have trails designated for runners, cyclists or walkers and places devoted to Recreation, Yoga or Crossfit. Since I am now looking forward to my 84th birthday in a few months I am especially interested in physical activity for seniors. I completed my last 50 miler when I was 65. Some of my friends are addicted to Silver Sneakers or Water Aerobics. In 2015 Harriette Thompson became the oldest woman to complete a 26.2-mile marathon. She ran with others in the Rock n Roll San Diego Marathon, finishing with a time of 7 hours, 44 minutes and 36 seconds at the age of 92. In the summer of 2015 the city of Broomfield, Colorado challenged people to walk 100 miles on a designated trail. Donna Agee, 90 years old, was awarded a commemorative T shirt after covering 25 miles of the course using her walker. All of this makes my experiences in running, which I share in the chapters of this book, more interesting.

. With Operation Nightwatch in Seattle

Late in 1969 a new program called "Operation Nightwatch" was starting in Seattle. In this ecumenical ministry local pastors from different churches were recruited to give one night a month. These volunteers wore the standard, white clergy collar as they walked the downtown streets and spent time in taverns. They became immediately available to people on the night scene. The founder of the program, Rev. Bud Palmberg, pastor of the Mercer Island Covenant Church, spent much more time on the night scene than those he recruited as volunteers. One night a strange sight unfolded on First Avenue before the shattering of glass from a large plate-glass window punctured the stillness of the evening.

Three burly men confronted Bud. These three muscular men were tossing the clergy collared man around in front of an adult book store which displayed a large picture of a buxom young woman, almost nude, as she held a seductive pose in a pole dance. Suddenly the clergy collar with man attached was tossed through the window of the store. Rev. Palmberg threw his right arm up to hide his eyes. He was not hurt seriously as he made his unexpected entry into the place of adult material.

The three who attacked him had been drinking. They probably saw him as someone out of his normal frame. Like broken glass from a window pane, he did not fit on the sidewalk in that part of town at that hour of the night. As a minister he was seen as someone normally bounded by a specific type of building, on a specific day of the week and by regularly scheduled services.

For clergy volunteering in Operation Nightwatch the night scene called for the learning of different behavior. Early in the Seattle program one of the volunteers had a unique learning experience while on duty. He walked into a tavern where some members of a local motorcycle club happened to be celebrating. As he approached one of these macho men who was wearing black leather pants and black leather jacket, he decided to extend a greeting he had observed two other men using in a different tavern. The reaction of the man dressed in black was immediate. He had a bicycle chain wrapped

Dean C. Jones

over his shoulders and over his ample belly. He uncoiled this chain, swung it in the air like a lasso, and caught the clergyman, knocking him to the floor. This nose to nose meeting with the hardwood floor of a tavern was not on the expected agenda for the minister. This volunteer discovered after the fact that he had insulted the macho man by using a greeting he had seen shared between two men in a gay bar. He was not physically hurt in this experience.

Early in my work for the Seattle program after I became a volunteer in 1979, I learned personally that the night scene can be unpredictable. At that time, I held a faculty position in the School of Nursing at the University of Washington. Operation Nightwatch used two rooms in an older Seattle hotel as an office back in 1979. One night the first Director of the program, Rev. Norm Riggins, asked me to open the office. As I approached the office on the second floor of this hotel I noticed that the cheap lock on the door had been forced open and that the door was ajar. I opened this door and when I stepped inside I saw a man, wearing a dark coat with large pockets and a brown hat with the front brim pulled down to hide part of his face. I caught him in the act of stuffing small items from the office into his pockets. When he saw me he brushed past me and out into the hall of the hotel. I followed him, asking why he would steal from a place that was only trying to help people. He then reached under his coat as I turned my back on him to return to the office where I intended to make a 911 call. His last words to me were "I'm gonna blast you."

For some reason this stranger changed his mind about shooting me and instead walked down the stairs and disappeared into the night. I was both surprised and felt fear as I stood alone in the empty hall of that old hotel. The stranger had effectively taken control of me, of the situation. This was foreign and uncomfortable for me. I had paid dues. I was the designated "leader" of this trip to the office. How could this strange man, obviously not in any way qualified to take charge of anything, proceed to command? This was part of my introduction to work that would engage my full-time attention for 20 years. The Seattle program is now under the Direction of Rev. Rick Reynolds.

I was never physically accosted while on duty in Seattle. I did learn a lot about a part of town that I was not familiar with. As I listened to men talk I heard stories about how a man who was beaten to death on the hill immediately north of Pike Place Public Market was simply rolled down the hill and shoved into an empty box car on the tracks below. The empty railroad car became a hearse, forever an accomplice in preserving the anonymity of the body and the killers as the train sped purposely and rabidly toward a destination far away from Seattle. Today luxury lofts, some selling for one million dollars, dot this hillside. It is, of course, off limits for the homeless. These luxury living places ride high above the ordinary dirt of the hillside. Residents cannot see the train tracks and have no interest in the sight of common freight trains chugging along mechanically. They can savor the sight of the constantly restless waters of the Puget Sound painted against the lovely background of the mountains of the Olympic Peninsula.

Another man died, not because of an altercation but because of his choice of where to sleep for the night. His last memory was a feeling of terror as he fell some 60 feet into the waiting arms of the waters of Puget Sound. This homeless man had decided to climb out on a wood beam under the structures along the waterfront. He must have decided that the two-foot-wide beam would be a safe place to sleep. But he rolled over in his sleep and became food for fish.

I was able to take a rare look at life on the streets of Seattle over 50 years ago as I talked with Howard. He was 61 at the time of our meeting, some 30 years ago. At that time, he had been part of the transient population for over 20 years. Howard was wearing a clean, brown leather jacket when we met. A silver cross hanging from a thin necklace caught my attention. He did not claim loyalty to any one church but spoke at length about his faith and sincere desire to help people. His helping became his way to connect.

It is impossible to look at how Howard helped others without considering his living accommodations. Howard slept in many different places around downtown Seattle over the years. He often walked as far south as the Spokane Street Viaduct to get away from the immediate downtown area at night. The longest period of time he could recall sleeping at one particular place was during the winter of 1978 when he stayed next to a wall not far from the sidewalk near the Downtowner Apartments on Fourth Avenue South. This was his "home" for four and one-half months.

This open-air space offered two levels for possible sleeping easily located without the services of a concierge. The most convenient spot was a ledge about two feet wide with an abrupt drop off of about 11 feet to the ground below. One night Howard took a free-fall off the ledge during his sleep. The next night he climbed down a tree to the lower level and set up a semi-permanent camp. Sheets of plastic protected him from the frequent baptism by the water-prone skies of Seattle. He could not be seen from the city streets. One day he was forced to re-locate when a city engineering crew bulldozed the area, uprooting his friendly tree and hauling away all of his personal property. During this unfriendly overture from the city Howard was donating his time to help paint a mission building, one of his ways to connect.

During our conversation Howard went into considerable detail about his primary occupation, picking up recyclable material on the streets of Seattle. His sage conclusion was that this full-time occupation was a very difficult way to come up with a few dollars. As he explained to me:

> "Time was when there were lots of wine bottles thrown away near downtown streets. I could collect some and magically transform them into cash at the rate of a penny a bottle. Back then I could buy a good breakfast for 35 cents. Now my work day starts at 5 AM and I stay at it most days until 9 PM. Some days I only make $5 for this long shift."

As Howard shared his view of life he said that it was important for him to help others, especially those with mental or physical disabilities. As I look back at my conversation with Howard I see that he talked about the very normal process of touching other people. This dance of engagement is important for everyone. This includes those we label as "mentally ill" or different in another way that moves them out of the comfortable norm. A month ago one of my brothers died. Norman had schizophrenia. From the age of 15 he had been cared for by the State. In the nursing homes his physical needs were met but I think that the staff could have done more to realize his need for association. I am afraid that I failed my brother as well in not realizing how much my visits meant to him. In spite of his delusions, he could always remember who I was.

One night when Howard was climbing down his tree to retire for the night he heard a noise from some near-by bushes. Looking closer he saw a man in the process of cutting his own throat with a long knife. The first slash of this knife drew some blood but was not fatal. The stranger was ready to make a deeper cut when Howard intervened. He hit the man intent on suicide on the chin, forcing the knife out of his hand. This man, carrying the knife, ran from the shrubbery. An Aid car later picked him up and gave him a free ride to the County Hospital. Howard was glad that he was able to prevent the unnecessary death but added that he was irritated because of the smear of blood on "his" wall.

On another night Howard reached out to a young Chinese couple who parked their car next to his sleeping place. He watched as the young man walked toward a parking meter to insert a coin. Before he could deposit the money Howard intervened to remind him that it was not necessary to pay for parking at that time of the night. He also told the couple that they did not need to worry about their car while they were dining, saying that he would look after it personally to make sure that no one broke into it. This couple was very impressed by Howard's generous concern for them. When they returned several hours later they called out to Howard and presented him with some special items of Chinese food plus a dollar bill. This exchange was a treasured memory for Howard.

What is the motivation for helping others? I thought of this question as Howard gave me a history lesson on mission activity in downtown Seattle. I walked with him back in time a number of years before our meeting when he sometimes visited a place called the Jericho Mission. This was located near First Avenue and Washington Street. Howard's memory of the place included a recollection of prolonged religious services, extending from 7 PM to 11 PM as the minister asked different "Sisters" and "Brothers" to give their testimony. Howard felt that street people were asked to go through too much "ear banging" just to get a night's lodging. At that time there were flop houses where a bed could be purchased for 35 or 50 cents a night. But some of these places were operated by drunks and were so dark or crawling with bugs that Howard did not feel comfortable sleeping in them.

Howard also recalled a mission run by Sister Dorothy years ago. This place was across the street from the main fire station. Sister Dorothy must have been a formidable sight on Seattle's Skid Row. Howard described her as a big woman, standing nearly six feet tall and weighing in excess of 200 pounds. Her physical bulk was accentuated by her strong, authoritarian personality. She demanded that the men coming to her mission sing during the service and also did not allow anyone to fall asleep during a service. Any sign of violating her rules resulted in the violator being immediately thrown out of the mission. One night when Howard was present a man went back for a second serving of food. When he later began to show signs that he would not be able to clean up his plate Sister Dorothy came up behind him and pushed his face down into the food. Howard recalled that Sister Dorothy was arrested several times by the police for her brutal treatment of the men who came to her mission.

On Occidental Street there was once a mission known as "The Cheese Mission." For Howard the best part of this mission was that religious services were always short. The Operator of the Mission simply read the 23rd Psalm. Each man present was then given a piece of cheese and a slice of bread. This place did charge for their services. During the 1960's a bed for the night could be purchased for 25 cents.

As he was recollecting about mission work in the past on Seattle's downtown streets Howard told me about a unique kind of activity. On Occidental Avenue a shapely young woman called Sister Faye and her attractive female partner both played the tambourine and sang gospel songs. It was Howard's conclusion that men on the street were more drawn by the physical appearance of these two women than by their attempts at evangelism. When these curvaceous tambourine planers collected a small amount of money they took a short break, going down the street to one of the taverns where they purchased drinks of wine to help fortify themselves for another round of music making on the street.

Many of my encounters with men and woman late at night were chance encounters for brief periods of time. There was seldom an opportunity to really know the details of anyone's life. But back when I was volunteering for the Seattle program I had an opportunity to talk at some length with Bill, a volunteer in the office. Bill was in his late 50's but looked much older. He told me that he had been introducing himself as an alcoholic at AA meetings for ten years. He attended AA meetings every week.

Bill lived in a modest two-room apartment a few blocks up from Seattle's downtown business district. He had many health problems; the most serious involved an abnormality in his heart and his total circulatory system. He survived on a monthly SSI check. He enjoyed singing in the choir in a small, downtown Lutheran Church. Bill never knew regular employment except for a period of three years in his early 20's when he was in the Army. He told me that he had been "in and out of more jails and detox places" than he could remember. He also had spent more time "on the street" than in rented housing.

From the age of 19 to the age of 55 Bill's periods of sobriety came primarily as a result of involuntary withdrawal from alcohol because of incarceration. He served three different prison terms for periods ranging from three to four years. Except for these years he recalled almost daily use of alcohol. He had his first drink at the age of 17. For a period of about two years he stopped at only one or two drinks per drinking episode. He first became intoxicated at the age of 19. His drink of choice from the age of 19 to 21 was Southern Comfort Whiskey. At about the age of 21 he switched from whiskey to "anything with alcohol in it." This included wine, beer, whiskey and a variety of products such as sterno and rubbing alcohol. He talked about long periods of time when he drank constantly, day and night.

The experience of going into the service was the trigger for Bill's first drinking spree. He was discharged from the Army because of his drinking. He claimed that drinking always made him feel "more confident," more "open" and more "relaxed." While drinking he could do things that he would never had been able to do without drink. This included having fun as well as breaking into stores and stealing.

For Bill his most extensive times of treatment came as part of his years in prison. In one particular prison he had easy access to a psychiatrist. This professional told Bill that he had a "pathological tendency to escape reality." The drinking was interpreted as one way to escape from the undesirable. From these encounters in prison Bill started to re-examine his relationships with people. He freely admitted to me that he had problems in letting people get too close to him. Although Bill had been through many detox experiences and the full range of missions he credited his sobriety to his own thinking. For him keeping sober was "not easy." It was most difficult for him at night when he was alone and faced with strong urges to drink.

A program reaching out at night must be ready to consider a wide range of possible problems. Sometimes the most pressing concern is the high risk of suicide. In Seattle the Operation Nightwatch program back in 1980 was able to offer a few hotel rooms to the homeless on a first come, first served basis when no other emergency space could be found in the city. Sometimes there was no opportunity to follow-up on the very difficult problems facing some of those who used these rooms. It was only after the fact that Rev. Norm Riggins became aware of the trauma an 18-year-old girl was going through. When one room was being prepared for a new guest the following few lines were found written on a scrap piece of paper in this room: They reflect the deep hopelessness of the young, temporary occupant. More importantly, they reflect the deep feelings of lots of people, young and old, who are caught in a "no-man's land" where all seems lost.

>To my friends I say goodbye
>Hoping they won't ask why.
>The pain is now too hard to take
>So I've chosen not to wake
>Life is hell, you can't win
>Giving up can't be a sin.
>Now my so-called friends do not weep.
>For my strength I no longer keep.
>I can't bear to think ahead
>Oh, how I wish I were dead.

If two apples are placed close together, touching, will the decaying skin of one affect the other? We know that people influence each other. Reaching out to help someone who has lost the desire to live is not a refreshing experience. But like showers from the sky that bless blighted plants as well as thriving rose bushes it must be done. Fr Don Erickson felt like a neglected and withering plant when I talked with him many years ago. His dream of outreach to the children on Seattle's streets was turning out to be a nightmare because he was finding it very hard to get financial support. As we shared cups of coffee together that I had purchased plus a slice of pie for him he was embarrassed by his freely flowing tears.

It is customary to think of new saplings in the forest as full of life. It is the "old growth" that can show the ravages of time, the signs of death from beetle or storm damage. Children are seen as "full of life," waiting for all that is to come. They are not generally regarded as potential victims for decay or death. Fr Erickson really struggled with his emotions as he shared with me his encounters around the suicide attempts of a 13-year-old boy, Stan. This boy was a frequent flyer on the downtown streets of Seattle. He was old enough to count, but he had been in so many foster homes that he had lost count. How does a boy with no family survive?

Stan fell into a pattern of using drugs, hustling people for money and petty theft. For him there was little to look forward to in life. He was around lots of pills, each calling to him seductively. In two serious suicide attempts this 13-year-old had feverishly ingested a large number of pills. He felt some power in being able to at least to try to bring an end to what had become impossible.

Unlike a death by hanging as in the case of celebrated actor and comedian Robin Williams in August of 2014, the taking of pills especially by a novice like a 13-year-old can be much more prolonged and uncertain in outcome. This is not something that anybody would purchase a ticket to watch. Fr Erickson shared with me his feelings around the long hours he spent watching a 13-year-old boy who was out of his mind from drugs and talking only about wanting to die.

One of the major problems for Fr. Erickson during this time was that the boy was a delinquent. Fr. Erickson knew that if he sought emergency services the boy would be immediately taken into custody. As part of his death trip, Stan sat for hours staring off into space while listening to the song, "The Rose" as sung by Bette Midler in the Mark Rydell film of that name.

"The Rose" has strong symbols of life and death as the song tells of a heart that is "afraid of breaking," about the fear of waking and refusing to take chances. It seems to be beckoning people to join a special fraternity of those not afraid of dying, the blessed who are not like those who fear death and thus never learn to live. The images of the song could be interpreted as pointing to death as good, as something that leads to better things like the seed dying in the winter to become a lovely rose in the spring. The words and the compelling melody captured the imagination of 13-year-old Stan.

Stan did survive his suicide attempts. He was placed in detention at the Juvenile Center in Seattle. Fr Erickson maintained contact with him. On one of his visits to this facility, Stan pleaded for a new pair of tennis shoes. Father Erickson was able to find the new shoes and presented them to Stan on his next visit. The boy then explained that he had walked in lots of places in his old shoes that he now felt ashamed about. I am sure that the bad places included much more than physical places along a sidewalk. They also included the marshy, unsavory places of emotional suffering and grief that he had known far in excess of what would be expected at his age. He wanted to start with new shoes, walking only where Jesus would be glad to see him walk.

The first experience with suicide in the Seattle program involved Rev. Palmberg. One night he was called to the scene as a young man edged out of a hotel room window threatening to jump. Bud made his way up to the room and talked to the man through an open window. When this man said that by jumping to the ground he could get his sister to listen to him Bud convinced him that in all likelihood the sister would never know about his death. A few minutes after this tense conversation the stranger crawled back into his room.

When Bud felt comfortable with the emotional state of the young man he went down to the hotel coffee shop for a cup of coffee. Before he could finish the coffee a hotel employee came rushing up to him. The man who had talked of suicide was reported to have locked the door to his room with shouts of "ending it all." Bud hurried back to the room. The hotel manager unlocked the door. Inside Bud found the man sprawled out on the floor, blood smeared over his body. He was trying to cut his wrists. Bud shoved the knife out of his grasp and used his tie as a bandage/tourniquet to stop the flow of blood before calling 911.

The man did survive his attempts at suicide. Bud visited him in the hospital. When he was released, Bud invited him to stay with a family in his church. Things seemed to be going along fairly smoothly. But when the family went on vacation the man set the house on fire. Bud and the members of his congregation did not immediately give up on the stranger. He was next invited to sleep in the church. One morning Bud was greeted by shouts coming through the locked door of his office. The man had locked himself in the room and had cut his wrists. He then collected some of the fresh blood in a paper cup and threw this at the books which lined the office. After this episode steps were taken to ensure that the man was admitted into a treatment facility. He never returned to the neighborhood of the church on Mercer Island. When last heard from he was in prison on charges of arson.

For me there is personal sadness in repeating this story. Years ago while teaching a sociology class in a community college I used the story as an illustration of suicide behavior. As I described the scene in the hotel room a young man in my class asked me not to be so graphic with the details. A woman in the class shared some of her own problems around the chronic health problems of her mother. I tried to be helpful regarding the parent but did not really talk with her about her own deep anxieties. Several months after the end of that school quarter I learned that this young woman who had completed my class took her own life in suicide. This makes me very aware of the need to take the topic seriously.

It is not easy to walk with someone who has lost all hope. Years ago when working to start an outreach program for Aberdeen, Washington I saw a man, trying to stand upright on the sidewalk but obviously bowed down not by the limited effects of some physical aliment but burdened by a very heavy load of depression. When I offered to give him a ride to an all-night store where he needed to buy something the heavy load lifted for a few moments. He had forgotten all of the vocabulary of joy. His constant companion was a truckload of feelings of loneliness. Some of his first words to me were… "I don't have any friends; I am all alone." He admitted that he had "cried so much" that he simply could no longer cry.

Dean C. Jones

Loss was the major baggage Kevin carried around from his near past. His wife left him. In Seattle, some 90 miles away from where I met him, Kevin had been living with his three daughters, the oldest nine years old. Flames from a major fire swept through the apartment building where they were living. Two of his precious girls died in this fire. Kevin was able to pull himself together enough to jump out the window, hugging his nine-year-old. He was with his lovely nine-year-old daughter until she was taken away from him and placed in a foster home after a judge determined that with his heavy use of alcohol he was not able to follow-through on the most basic needs of the young girl. Now he was wandering the streets of a town far from Seattle. His final plea to me was that he did not want anyone, especially his little girl, to know that he was "dying like this." He was preoccupied with thoughts of death because he had been told that he was, in fact, dying of AIDS, contracted when he used dirty needles in his urgent need to get a fast reaction from the taking of illegal drugs. In my car, before the curtain of life was pulled over him, Kevin had a rare opportunity to experience something very special to him. He had been a professional musician. I became an audience as he drummed out a tune on the dash of the car and sang a song he had never had a chance to perform before. He wrote the words for his wife:

> I thought about you all night long
> Couldn't get no sleep.
> We used to have a love so right
> My love was oh so deep.
> Oh, must have been a year or so
> Since I laid eyes on you.
> I've been so miserable,
> I've been so blue.
> Oh, everybody keeps asking me
> Why I feel this way.
> In my mind I can't be free
> Till you come home to stay.
> Oh, I threw away your picture
> I tried to forget you.
> In my mind I hear you laugh
> Lord, What can I do?

On one rainy night in Seattle I carried a black umbrella as I ducked into a downtown tavern I had visited before. After shaking out excess water and folding the umbrella I sat at the bar and ordered a glass of Coke. In a few minutes two men came through the front door of this place, followed by a burst of cold wind. Both of these men carried large back packs. One man was average in height. His buddy was tall and thin. This second man used the street name of "Too Tall." From their appearance and mannerisms, I assumed that these two were strangers in town.

As it turned out, the shorter of the two strangers, Bob, sat down on a bar stool next to me. When he noticed my clergy collar he was friendly, offering to buy me a Coke. We talked. Over the course of a few minutes I learned that the two had arrived in town in an empty boxcar, courtesy of the Burlington Northern and Santa Fe railroad. They had heard of temporary work near Portland, cutting Christmas trees. The switching yard for trains going to Portland was some 20 miles south of Seattle near Auburn. They had considered hitchhiking, but the heavy rain made this a very difficult prospect. I listened to both men for some time before deciding that I would offer them a ride.

When I mentioned a free ride to Auburn, these two strangers left a half-empty pitcher of beer on the bar, gathered up their back packs and followed me out of the tavern. Outside I held my umbrella overhead as we loaded the back-packs into the trunk of my car. Then the shorter man slid into the middle of the front seat while Too Tall sat next to the door on the passenger's side as I drove south out of Seattle, the windshield wipers trying to keep up with the torrents of rain.

Bob talked for the first few minutes before the warmth and steady motion of the car lulled him to sleep. His talk was all about the experience of spending time in "every detox and jail on the West Coast." Too Tall asked if he could "play the radio." He then proceeded to switch from station to station over the range of the dial, acting like a kid with a new Christmas toy, until he found a country western station. We drove through the darkness with the music playing at high volume. At one point I was not sure which road to take. I asked Too Tall if he knew where to go. He said that he had never been south of Seattle by car.

Somewhere along the way Too Tall said that he really wanted to see a dog that a friend was keeping for him. I followed his directions as we turned off the Interstate to drive down lonely, dirt roads. We found the house that Too Tall recognized but there was no dog. He did not want to disturb the people in the house. When we were far from other cars on seldom traveled back roads Too Tall informed me that he was on probation for murder. I did not see this as the best place or time for such an announcement! As he explained the situation, a man in the freight yard in Spokane, Washington tried to steal something from his bags. Knives were pulled and Too Tall cut the man who later died in the Emergency Room of a local hospital. The court action accused Too Tall but also recognized a measure of self-defense. I was certainly not made comfortable with the knowledge that I was driving down back roads in the dark with someone holding a conviction for murder.

We did get back to the Interstate. I was able to find the location in Auburn where these men wanted to go. They were very thankful for the ride. Too Tall gave me a Seattle bus transfer and a pair of sun glasses he had found on the street as "payment" for the help. I did not learn much about what it is like to ride the rails. I did have the experience of sharing a few hours with two men who were very thankful for a helping hand in the middle of the night. Two men made it to their destination where they would wait to catch a freight train to Portland. I would also soon be going to Portland to begin my journey in night ministry beyond Seattle.

With a PhD in sociology and experience in college teaching why did I turn to the challenges of night ministry for 20 years of my life? As one way to promote and fund my work I completed 50 mile runs and a 72 mile run around Lake Tahoe. In the next chapter I go back to my childhood and to my first attempts at running. Hopefully this will answer some of the questions about why I took strange turns in my life.

Operation Nightwatch in Seattle – Update

Operation Nightwatch remains a strong presence in Seattle after nearly 50 years. Under the direction of the present Director, Rev. Rick Reynolds, the program has seen major growth. A web site and monthly newsletter share stories and pictures of the work. In sharing about the history of this work insightful comments include an account of the beginning of the program back in 1969 when Rev. Bud Palmberg first ventured into the downtown core of Seattle at night. In 1999 property was purchased at 302 14th Ave. S. The first floor of this building is a Dispatch Center. The upper two floors are used as rental housing for 24 low-income seniors. The present mailing address for the program is: P.O. Box 21181, Seattle, WA 98111. Rick can be reached on the internet at: rick@seattlenightwatch.org.

A good summary of the program is contained in a mission statement which is shared on the web site:

Operation Nightwatch is an interdenominational Christian ministry serving the poor and homeless in order to help people to obtain their highest level of self-reliance. The program provides:

• Spiritual care and hope for the community at night.

• Compassionate relief and shelter placement for homeless men, women and children.

• Low-cost housing and support services for seniors and the disabled.

• Education and encouragement for others to respond to those in need.

Chapter 2

From the Starting Line in Ministry and Running

Ministry

Many threads of my life were woven together to enable me to give 20 years of my life to downtown ministry at night. I was born in 1932 during the dark days of the Great Depression. My father, Henry, found it very hard to find any kind of work. Those were the days when long lines of men waited patiently, hoping for a loaf of bread. Popular songs included lyrics like "Brother, Can You Spare a Dime." New organizations like the CCC and the WPA became life lines for many. My father was ill prepared for the competition for jobs. He did not finish High School and had no special work skills. In the year of my birth he had given up. Instead of looking hopelessly for work he went through a long spell when he spent most of his time in a local movie theatre all day long. At this low ebb in his life his older sister, Dovie, urged him to go to church with her. She was attending the First Church of God in Denver, Colorado. Dad went to church with her and his life was changed. He started looking for work and did find a paying job to feed his growing family which ultimately included five boys. From that day on the Church became a very important part of his life and also the life of our family.

The major brush stroke that changed life for my father and for our family did not wipe out the curves and bumps on the road of life for me. When I was seven we moved to Seattle, Washington and then to Edmonds, Washington. In a large family you always look up the tree to compare yourself to others. I felt that I was a minor branch compared to my older brother, Darold. He seemed to do everything right, in the church and in school. He was youth leader in church and student body president in High School. I was only an also ran. As I began to crawl out of my shell I tried to navigate the rocky road of adolescence. This was not an easy task for me. Family rules made it harder. We were not allowed to go to the movies or to attend school dances.

When I was 17, I did something that never appears on the roster of accomplishments for any family member. It is never a topic of conversation at family reunions. At the time we were living in a large house on 6 and ½ street in downtown Edmonds, Washington. Dad had moved up the work ladder to become a real estate broker. This was several rungs up from his previous work as a house painter and paper hanger. The seven of us lived in a five-bedroom house with Mom and Dad taking the bedroom on the first floor and the four bedrooms upstairs reserved for the boys. My younger brothers, Norman and Arthur, shared a large bedroom. Dwaine, Darold and I all had our own bedrooms. Live was moving along at a predictable pace.

I can only imagine the fear for my folks one morning when the normal fall of footsteps on the stairs was short one pair of shoes. Mom would have been in the kitchen, preparing breakfast for the family. The odor of freshly fried bacon and eggs would drift upstairs. But I did not smell or see the cozy scene around the breakfast table. I was not around and no one knew where I was. I had decided to run away from home. At 17 I had saved a little money from my work in a tree nursery where I made $1 an hour. I put a few things in a bag and crawled out of my bedroom window at night. I did not know where I would go, just wanted to be out on my own. I had decided to hitch-hike to someplace far away. My first task was to get out of Edmonds to find a major highway. I had no experience in the fine art of standing by the side of the road with a thumb out as cars passed. I did get to a major interstate. I know that I must continue with the telling of this story, but it is not easy. I stayed away from home for about two weeks. I never phoned and never left a message when I ran away. Both of my parents have now been dead for several years. They both loved each of their boys. They did not deserve the pain I threw their way.

The year was 1949. Our country had endured through costly wars in Europe and the Far East. Everyone had become familiar with the friendly voice of the Chief Executive in the Oval Office giving his regular "fireside chats." The country was marching ahead to a new time of industrial expansion and peace. I had been through air-raid drills as an elementary school student in Seattle. We lived in a large rented house near Green Lake. After the move to Edmonds I attended Edmonds High School where I opted for some of the most difficult courses including Algebra, Geometry and Chemistry. I was a good student. I also worked hard in the tree nursery owned by Mrs. Narron. I learned how to use a spade and a hoe. She never adopted mechanized tools. When a large plot of ground needed to be "plowed" she handed me a shovel. I walked a mile to and from work.

In spite of what I had done, I was on shaky grounds in terms of who I was as a person in relation to others. In my family there was never a "fireside chat." Everyone was busy, doing his or her own thing. Mom and Dad worked hard to cover the basic needs of a large immediate family plus extended family members when this became necessary. At 17 I should have been dating. Instead I was on a major interstate highway hoping for a ride. Drivers along a highway can see who they are approaching. They can make a decision about where and when to stop. Anyone who tries to hitch a ride has forfeited the power to decide who to ride with. Any ride offer is appreciated.

Dean Jones in 1949

Late in the day on the first day of my journey away from home I was alone on a lonely stretch of highway in southern Washington when a green pick-up truck stopped in response to my thumbs-up signal. At that time the front seat of most vehicles fostered community, allowing for three people to sit beside each other. After I climbed up into the front seat I saw that my companions were a man and a woman. He was wearing a ball cap; she was in casual dress. After climbing in to sit beside the woman and closing the door on the passenger's side I listened to the flow of words between the others in the cab. Words are like arms, reaching out to connect people. This man and woman had a good relationship. I was all alone with no one to talk to. From their conversation I learned that they were married. They talked about their children. They knew where their children were. I am sure that they had no worry about one of their children someday deciding to run away from home. As the pick-up hurried down the road, taking me farther away from my home, darkness was approaching. The warmth of the day was fading into night. This only increased my own sense of being truly alone, far from my comfortable bed, far from the familiar sounds of a family in motion.

It was at this point that I received a gift from a stranger. With my height of six feet I assume that this couple took me for someone older than 17 when they stopped to give me a ride. As my eyes began to close in the cab of that pick-up the woman looked directly at me and then made a comment to her husband...."why, he's only a kid." The sympathy in her voice touched me. My hitch-hiking adventure was becoming a dance of association. The kindness from strangers at night became one of the motivations for me to get involved in helping others at night many, many years later.

It is not possible to plan exactly where you are going when you depend on the energy of others to move you along the highway. As a hitch-hiker you really have no place on the carefully groomed, hard, asphalt highway. It is engineered for heavy car and truck traffic. Your presence is an affront to the purposeful, sometimes high speed, movement of people and machines. Some days after my chance meeting with the couple in Washington I found myself near a small town in Nevada. Again, it was late in the day. I did hold my thumb out, begging for a ride. But there wasn't much traffic. As the sun abandoned the day to rest beyond the horizon I walked into the small town. My body was giving me the message that it was time to sleep. A commercial building on one of the main streets of this Nevada town called out to me.

This building did not offer a bed with cozy blankets. But it was off the sidewalk and displayed a window-free space large enough for me to stretch out on the ground in the darkness. Shortly after I was beginning to adopt this space as a temporary shelter I was approached by a policeman. He abandoned his primary calling to issue tickets and make arrests. Instead he was simply concerned about my safety. This man, wearing a wide-brimmed hat, a badge and a service revolver, spoke softly as he told me that no one was being held in the local jail that night. He invited me to go with him a short distance to the jail where, he said, I could sleep free of charge for the night. I walked with him, entering a small jail cell where I spent the night on a cot with the door unlocked. Another example of how I was helped, not hurt, on my journey and another precursor of my own work at night.

All journeys must come to an end. My adventure, using my thumb as a means of transportation, ended somewhere in Texas. I can't recall the name of the city. I do remember having enough money to pay for a room in a hotel for the night. This was a Saturday night. On Sunday I went to a church nearby and vowed to return home and also to begin to consider going into the ministry. Following the time in church I was again on the road, hoping that someone would help me get home. My first objective was to get to California and then to thumb my way up the coast to Washington.

Out on the highway I watched as cars sped by, hurrying to places of work, going somewhere with somebody in mind. Again I was a loner, a twist of seaweed on the shore of normal life. Lost in these feelings, I almost neglected to notice that a car had pulled to a stop a few feet from me. When I hurried to this car and opened the door on the passenger side of the front door I glanced over and was surprised to see a middle-aged, large, Black man. He chatted with me as the car moved on down the road.

After a few hours passed it became time to consider getting something to eat. My Black tour guide stopped in the parking lot of a restaurant and gave me some money, telling me to go in and get food for both of us. We ate in the car. It was only after the fact that I realized that at that time in that part of Texas a Black person might not be welcomed to sit comfortably inside with "normal" patrons. Later it became time when most travelers would be looking for a motel or hotel space for a good night's sleep. Again I knew that the race of the driver made him a non-welcome entity at some of the motels which lined the interstate. We drove through the night, all night long before reaching California where I was again deposited along the highway. I had been given much more than a free ride; I was again blessed by the help of another stranger in the night.

A few months after my delinquent journey from Washington to Texas and back I was in Anderson, Indiana to enroll at Anderson College as a freshman. It was now 1950 and I was 18. Before classes began I found a full-time job at a local General Motors plant, knowing that I would need to cover all of my own college expenses. I worked on the evening shift in a plant making auto horns on an assembly line. The men who worked with me were supporting families on our salary of $2.85 an hour. During my college years the only gift I received from home was a box of cookies mailed to me from Mom. Most of them were broken in transit. But they were much appreciated. They had been baked and mailed with lots of love.

When I left home for the second and last time I had bus fare and a little money saved from my work in the tree nursery. I rode a Greyhound bus from Seattle to Anderson, Indiana. In addition to my full-time work off campus another extra-curricular activity that was not complimentary to the normal learning in college was marriage. Out in Washington I had met a girl at a church camp meeting. This girl, Stella, (actually a woman of 21 when I was 18) came back to Anderson to see me over the Christmas break. I proposed, we were married and I moved out of the dorm. It would have been more normal for me to date at that age, discovering more about myself in relation to girls. But this was not possible, I was married.

At the General Motors plant I sat in a booth from 4PM to 12 midnight testing auto horns. I picked up a horn from the belt running in front of me and applied it to electric terminals to see if it had the correct sound. If not, I sent it back up the line to be fixed. This is not exactly what the first year of college should be like. I did not know about fraternity parties or times with friends in the evening. I did take a full load of classes but contacts with students were confined to the classroom. Stella and I remained in Anderson for the rest of the school year but then the call of the West was too strong. We returned to the West Coast, going to Portland, Oregon where I finished my first undergraduate degree at Pacific Bible College (now Warner Pacific College).

When we moved to Portland I soon found a job working at night in a machine shop. During one summer break I actually held two full-time jobs for a few weeks. There was no time for and no interest in running. At PBC I was fortunate to have some very good professors. Three who stand out in my memory were; Irene Caldwell, Milo Chapman and Otto F. Lynn. Dr. Irene Caldwell taught Christian Education, using a book she had written as a text. Dr. Milo Chapman specialized in the Old Testament. He had attended a seminary in Berkeley and brought some of the latest scholarly work on the Old Testament to his classes. Dr. Otto F. Lynn was an expert in New Testament Greek. He was one of the scholars who worked on the translation resulting in the Revised Standard Version of the Bible. Beyond his scholarly ability, he was a truly good person. I was one of his last students. He developed Parkinson's disease and this made him retire early.

My full-time work off campus in Portland introduced me to a very new world. One of my jobs was on the night shift at Fowler Manufacturing Company. I wore heavy gloves and lifted heavy sheets of steel during my 8-hour shift from 4PM to midnight. This work called for the use of my whole body. It was not like sitting at a desk in class or in the library. I operated machinery, primarily punch presses. In my job I was a team manager, working with an assistant to lift the sheets of steel up into a punch press. These strong sheets of steel would become the inner core of hot water heaters, the end product of the operation.

Manufacturing has declined markedly in our country. Some processes are automated while others have been shipped off shore. Students in college today use the products made by others. They do not produce things. In classes teachers must compete with lap-top computers. Cell phones, smart phones and other devices are part of everyday life. Not many today can point to an object and say that they had a part in its manufacture.

One of the busiest times for me during my college years were the years I spent in the graduate program in sociology at the University of Washington. The full time student role including time for the research and writing of my MA thesis and PhD dissertation was complimented with again nearly 40 hours of work off campus. At that time my two children were in school and my wife was also a PhD student at the University of Washington.

I know that I am blessed in being able to sit at a word processor to type out these words with the added advantage of spell check. I did hitch hike from Seattle to somewhere in Texas and back. Then and now this kind of activity has a potential for personal harm. I was never hurt, only helped by strangers. At Fowler Manufacturing I worked with powerful machines which could cut steel as well as body parts. Late one night I heard a scream and knew that someone had been hurt. The punch presses sometimes double-tripped. If a hand was in the press cleaning out scraps from a prior down-thrust of the press this hand became a prime target. The scream I heard that night came from Vince, a young man who was working at night while taking classes during the day to become a mechanic. The punch press took three fingers of his right hand. I had no contact latter with Vince but have wondered how or if he managed to pursue his dream of becoming a mechanic. My work at night in ministry was done in the part of town where it was not unusual for people to be seriously hurt or killed. But I was never injured. I do not take the pages of this chapter or the sharing in other chapters for granted. I have the use of both hands. I have been blessed in the experiences I have had and in being able to share them near the end of my life.

Pastor of the Church of God in Rainier, Oregon:

After graduation from Pacific Bible College with a degree in Bible and Theology I was ordained and then invited to serve the Church of God in Rainier, Oregon. Rainier is near the free-flowing waters of the Columbia River. The Columbia does not require money to maintain its regular, natural flow. Since a pastor is seen as living close to the Divine, the origin of all things natural, it should follow that he/she should also flow along with little worry about such mundane issues as what to eat and where to sleep. The Rainier Church of God was a small congregation. The town depended largely on a sawmill. I was paid a "salary" of $50 a week and given free use of a parsonage for myself and my wife. I was given no health insurance and no contributions were made to a pension fund. Lewis Vale, a leader in the church, carefully explained that this salary was representative of the money earned by men in the congregation. He also said that I would be expected to give full time to the church. No work on the side would be permitted.

Before moving into the parsonage I took on the solo task of re-decorating the front room of the parsonage. I was re-directing long strips of green wallpaper to their ultimate destination on one wall when someone knocked on the front door. Responding to this knock, I opened the door to find a young man standing on the front porch, trying to hide his tears. When I invited him in he said that his youngest child, his favorite, had died and that he wanted me to do the funeral service. I was 22 at the time. I had never attended a funeral service, but I offered to help him. After he left I walked over to the large Methodist church in town and borrowed a book on funerals from the pastor. I did my best in the service as I stood behind the closed casket at the front of my church as a few family members and friends joined me for the occasion.

Officiating at funerals became an important duty for me in Rainier. I did this every other month, primarily for people in the community. Only one service was for a member of my congregation. As the pastor my primary duty was to come up with two unique sermons every Sunday, one for a morning service and another for an evening service. I was also the leader of the mid-week prayer service on Wednesday evening. In addition to these formal duties I was expected to visit members of the congregation. Some lived out of town on farm property. No one had ever heard of mileage reimbursement. I was young and busy so spent little or no time worrying about the long-range financial implications of my work as a minister.

One of my most memorable contacts in Rainier was with an older couple who lived across the street from the parsonage. The woman was very ill. Every time I visited with them her husband would give her a "hot toddy" in a tall glass. He said that the drink was heavily laced with alcohol and that it was essential to keep her going. I happened to be present when she died. The local mortician came by himself to pick up the body. I helped him carry her out to the hearse. I was glad that I was around to do this. It would have been unfortunate if the husband had been pressed into doing this job.

The mortician ran a very tight ship in terms of expenditures. He was also a very controlling person. He took charge of me in my own church, marching me down the center aisle toward the casket. I never did a memorial service. There were no cremations in those days. I always stood just above the casket with family members gathered near.

Normally there is little personal contact between the process of maintaining a comfortable temperature inside a house and the residents of the house. The primary decision for a homeowner is which finger to use in touching the automatic temperature control switch. In the parsonage in Rainier I was invited to become intimately involved with the maintaining of the interior temperature which was a real challenge during cold winter days and nights. The house was heated with a sawdust burning furnace in the basement.

I was a frequent caller to the local sawmill. For a small fee they dispatched a large dump-truck of sawdust which was unceremoniously dumped on the front yard of the parsonage. The house came gifted with a large wheelbarrow and a sturdy shovel. I shoveled sawdust into the obliging wheelbarrow, pushed this load into the basement and unloaded it. A large metal hopper sat, always hungry, near the furnace. I helped the sawdust move from a pile on the floor into its ultimate destination in the hopper. An auger ran under this refuge for sawdust, carrying it into the furnace proper. I wheeled a lot of sawdust during the winter. This activity was not covered by classes in Bible School. One of the serendipitous offerings given by a sawmill is the high probability of a chimney or roof fire from the bright, glowing embers of burning sawdust. One evening we were awakened by the sound of a fire truck pulling up in the front of the house. The wood-shingled roof had caught fire and someone alerted the local fire department. Fortunately, the blaze was extinguished before any major damage was inflicted.

One function of a house is to serve as a barrier from unwanted outside intrusion. But the personal space of the parsonage in Rainier was invaded twice during our tenure. One summer evening we left a window open in the upstairs bedroom. In the middle of the night I heard a loud banging against one wall. Turning on a light I disturbed a bat in its attempt to get back to normal habitat. I was able to get a large broom and with this I forced closure on the bat's retreat out the window. Then I closed the window.

On another occasion I was giving our new-born son, Steven, a bath in his Bathinette in the kitchen one morning. I had turned on the stove in this kitchen to provide a better source of heat than the ambitious but unpredictable sawdust burning bemouth living in the basement. Steven was born during our time in Rainier. The morning bathing ritual was interrupted that morning when I heard a noise under the kitchen sink. When I opened the doors below the sink I surprised a large river rat. He/she scurried away. Since the house was not far from the river this kind of incursion should have been expected. The sewer line into the house became an expressway for adventurous rats. We had only one visit of this type.

Of course the church experience for me in Rainier was much more than the challenges of living in a house near the river. The people in the congregation were my main focus. Most of the men worked in the local sawmill. Some put in 8 hour shifts pulling lumber off a green chain after round logs were converted into marketable lumber by a large saw. Other men became expert in manipulating a fork-lift truck around the yard. A few in the congregation were engaged in other kinds of work. One family, for example, owned the primary furniture store in town.

In a small, rural church it is not unusual for the pastor to become familiar with parishioners in ways not fostered by church assignments in large cities. Duane and Charlotte Patching were leaders in the church. Duane worked at the sawmill but he also did some farming. He owned a few acres where he harvested hay every summer. One summer he asked me to help him. I rode with him out of town on a tractor. A flat-bed trailer obediently followed the tractor. My job was to tackle fairly large bales of hay and then to throw them up into the slow-moving trailer.

I knew that the Rainier assignment would not be long lived. I could not see how my limited income would meet the needs of a growing family. Stella did get a job across the river at Longview Fiber that gave us much needed supplemental funds. But I resigned my position after two years. We moved first to Portland, Oregon where I took additional classes in Christian Education. During this time our second child, Kathy, was born. I then accepted a call to another small, rural church in Oregon in the town of Baker (now Baker city).

Pastor of the Church of God in Baker, Oregon:

Baker was one of the stops on the old Oregon Trail back when the west was being developed. For me it was a stop on my way to college teaching, night ministry and the very difficult task of sharing memories on these pages.

The pull of Baker for me was that it came with the promise of making a little more money. I was promised a salary of $38 a week but in contrast to Rainier, I was told that I could work on the side.

My family of four was given a few rooms attached to the rear of the church as a place of residence. The congregation was again very small. After I left they tried to grow with a new building but the venture failed and today there is no Church of God in Baker City.

In Baker I had new learning experiences with no relation to the Bible School curriculum. My major job out of the setting of the church was to work as a beginning carpenter for Carl Peterson. He was a leader in the church and also a very good builder. I was invited to participate in all phases of home construction from building the wood forms to embrace the heavy serving of freshly poured concrete that would become the footings for a house to securing asphalt shingles as the final state of construction. Nailing the wood studs together which became the main skeleton of the house was an interesting process as well as the work in securing sheet rock to the frame and nailing down narrow strips of hardwood flooring.

I did have a small office in the church. But there wasn't much time to use this space. I was busy working to supplement my limited income. The church was not able to pay me more. There were some Sundays when the church treasurer, Lorraine Valentine, told me to hold my check until late on Monday so that she would have time to deposit the money from the collection on Sunday. I am not sure what difference I made for those who sat in the small church Sunday after Sunday. I tried to do my best with my limited background and limited resource material in the small office. I resigned and moved to Seattle after only three years.

In Seattle I first enrolled in Seattle Pacific University where I received a BA in sociology with Dr. Mel Foreman as my mentor. I then went on to the University of Washington where I earned an MA and a PhD in sociology. This gave me access to teaching positions for 13 years. It was during my tenure in academic positions that I began my long distance running. That was also when I returned to Seattle again and held a position at the School of Nursing at the University of Washington. While holding this position I volunteered in Seattle's Operation Nightwatch, as I mentioned in the last chapter, and then began my 20 years of full time service in different cities at night.

Running

I first started reminiscing about my running some 14 years ago. At the time I was living in Seattle and often ran the 2.9-mile distance around Green Lake, a truly pristine spot in the throbbing metropolis of the city. On a Saturday morning in December I pulled on my Gortex running pants and jacket, designed to provide an artificial layer of protection from the cold and rain. Then I put on a thick pair of Thurlo socks. These blue and gray socks came with a series of three protective zones patented to cushion the reality of hard concrete. As the impact zone, shear zone and control zone hugged my feet and ankles I considered a slight discomfort in my right arch and trusted that the manufactured denial of the results of years of running would be effective. The last part of my uniform against the naked concrete and outside cold were my running shoes. My feet were forced into a pair of size 11 Asics running shoes recently purchased at the Super Jock and Jill store near Green Lake. These $100 cradles for feet came with a tough cushioned sole and a thin inner sole that was removable. At the age of 69 I appreciated each and every one of the technological buffers against the realities of running on city streets in winter.

When I was training for my first 50 miler I sometimes ran around Green Lake 12 times for my near 36-mile work-out, passing every runner on the trail in the process. Then years later my parents lived in a senior residence a few miles from the lake. I have good memories of running from their place to the lake and then around the lake once or twice. They have now been dead for a number of years.

When I first walked out my front door for an attempt at running I was a new transplant to Salt Lake City, anxious to begin my teaching career at a major university a far distance from the familiar sights and sounds of Seattle. I held the title of Assistant Professor of Sociology at the University of Utah. Fresh from my graduate work at the University of Washington, I had not yet completed the defense of my doctoral dissertation, giving me the dubious title of "All but Dissertation." Or ABD. An attractive, young Mormon woman working near campus offered to type my completed dissertation as the first part of its journey to a final resting place in the dead book section of the main library at the University of Washington. She said that she would do the typing for a modest fee plus the opportunity to have dinner with me. I am not sure what my motivation was back then, but for the first time in my life I was trying to grow a full beard. I took my stubble of beard and my anxiety about dining with a strange woman while I was married to the faculty lounge for the "dinner date." The small talk turned around her interest in a man who was out of town at the time. I left her early in the evening at our meeting place on campus and went home to my two children. My wife, Stella, was back in Seattle at the time, working on her own dissertation.

Stella and I plus our two children, now teen-agers, were treated well in Salk Lake City where we lived in a large house rented from a Mormon Bishop. I was worried about finances after the long and expensive time of graduate school ending with both my wife and me earning the PhD. I am not sure what prompted me to go over to a near-by High School track for a few minutes of running. This was the first time in years that I had any free time. My undergraduate and graduate years always came with full-time or near full-time work.

I did not become serious about running in the city settled by Mormons after Brigham Young proclaimed "This is The Place!" from an over-look provided by the Wasatch Mountains. One of my personal goals was to run into Temple Square but on the Saturday morning of this attempt I ate too much for breakfast and was also in poor shape so I aborted the effort after a mile or two.

After only one year at the University of Utah I accepted a position at Indiana-Purdue University at Indianapolis (IUPUI). One of the main attractions was an offer of a teaching post for my wife at Indiana Central University in the same city. Shortly after arriving in the city dubbed "a cornfield with lights" I again started running in a well-worn pair of tennis shoes. At that time, I was 39 and facing what I considered to be a very undesirable place to live. Indiana was too far from the water and mountains of Washington State. One of my joys was running. I started a regular schedule calling for an hour of running every morning.

My most serious marathon running and college teaching years covered the time from 1972 to 1987 or from my age of 40 to 55. This included my last years at Indianapolis where I lived for six years before moving to Winston-Salem, North Carolina for a three-year appointment at the Bowman Gray School of Medicine and then ended my college teaching career in 1987 at the University of Washington.

Running Awards

During those years I followed a precise weekly schedule of 10 miles a day, off one day and then a 20-mile work-out in preparation for my Marathon runs. When I started running 50 mile events my long weekly run became 36 miles. How do you tell the story of runs long ago? Far from the hard-packed pavement, the sight of freshly plowed farm fields, the feel of energy as your feet keep up a regular beat, mile after mile. I have forgotten much of the detail in races now over 40 years old. I did not keep an accurate log of my running events. From awards and the remains of memorabilia I can reconstruct some of my achievements. I have no idea why I decided to enter a marathon in North Carolina nor how I managed the expense of getting there. But I hold a plague that confirms my presence at the Charlotte Observer Marathon in December of 1972. Usually I found myself in the middle of the pack of runners. This time my effort earned me a time of 3 hours and 17 minutes. That same year I was again in the middle of the stream of runners on a very hot June day in Toledo, Ohio. This city was best known for many glass manufacturing operations. That day the main attraction was a marathon, aptly named the Glass City Marathon. I completed this event with a finish time of 3 hours, 26 minutes and 36 seconds.

As you will see in my sharing of specific events, it is the surround of circumstances around a run as well as the run itself which helps form the memory capsule of a given event. I recall Detroit, Michigan primarily because my wife's cousin, Rodney and his wife, Dawn, lived in that city while he was working for General Motors. We stayed with them when I drove up from Indianapolis to enter the Belle Isle Marathon. I was anxious to run this event because I knew that the course was flat with no hills to endanger a good running time. On October 27, 1974 I ran the marathon at Belle Isle with a time of 3 hours and 4 minutes, my best marathon time. In the same year I also ran the 3rd annual Marathon-Marathon in Terre Haute, Indiana in 3 hours and 21 minutes. That same year I also completed a marathon in the college town of Whitewater, Wisconsin. The Whitewater event merits comments later in this chapter.

The Boston Marathon is generally seen correctly as the keystone of any marathon running career. It is now impossible to think of the Boston without recalling the horrors of 2013 when a noble finish area became the scene of unthinkable carnage after a home-made bomb was deliberately detonated to produce the most injury. Three people were killed and over 260 injured, some very seriously. There were no bombs and no thought of potential terrorist back in 1975 when I finished my first Boston Marathon in 3 hours, 18 minutes and 28 seconds. In 1978 at the age of 45 I managed to again get to Boston, staying with someone known to a member of the faculty at Bowman Gray School of Medicine. That Boston event turned out to be my best—ever Boston Marathon with a time of 3 hours, 7 minutes and 45 seconds.

During that time, I was entering and completing a number of events. In October of 1977 I posted a 3 hour and 10-minute time at the 2nd annual Greensboro, North Carolina Marathon. In addition to the Boston in 1978 I completed the "Run for Heart" 10 kilometer race in Salisbury, North Carolina with a time of 40 minutes and 52 seconds. Also in 1978 I completed the Wake Forest University ROTC run of 7 miles in Winston-Salem, North Carolina in 47 minutes and 25 seconds. At the age of 62 I ran the Trails End Marathon in Seaside, Oregon with a time of 3 hours and 45 minutes, giving me first place for my age division. I have now finished seven runs of 50 miles, the first in Seattle, Washington on October 13, 1979 in 7 hours and 14 minutes. My last 50 miler was at the age of 65 when I ran the distance in 8 hours and 35 minutes. My longest run was the 72 mile Pepsi of Reno run around Lake Tahoe on September 18, 1981.

Back when I was teaching I made it a practice to run in strange cities when going to a professional meeting. The high rise mountains of concrete, glass and steel grudgingly giving up earth space to pedestrians and cars in downtown New York City is a very different place to run on a Sunday afternoon than out along the levies near Bourbon Street in New Orleans or on sidewalks near the grass and tress of park spaces in San Francisco.

During a sociology meeting in San Francisco I decided to run across the Golden Gate Bridge. Selecting a day with few presentations of interest to me, I drove out of the parking lot at the Hilton Hotel and west in the direction of the Bridge. Finding what I considered to be a good place to leave the car, I parked it on the street, locked the doors and headed off running. As I ran I asked for directions. I was given conflicting accounts of the best bridge approach. In the process I found myself lost in a strange town. After running through the Embarcadero, I finally made it to the high superstructure of the famous Golden Gate Bridge. Seeing this sight and the view out over the Bay, Alcatraz Island and downtown San Francisco it is hard not to think of the famed Birdman of Alcatraz and others who woke up every morning aware that their day would not include free running on the city streets or any other expression of freedom. Running the bridge was a major accomplishment for me since I have a fear of heights.

At the northern edge of the bridge I spotted a young woman standing alone with a camera. I stopped just enough to ask if she would take my picture and gave her my address to send it to. Several weeks later I got the picture but also a long letter in which she made it obvious that she wanted to begin some kind of relationship. I never considered a sweaty runner as an object of interest. I did not respond to the writer of the letter.

My fondest memories of relationships sparked by running are around two dogs who became very special to me. In Greenville,

Illinois I ran through farming country soon after leaving the city limits. One day I noticed a large German Shepherd dog sitting patiently at the approach to a small bridge. I made a big detour around this strange sight and continued my long run. Coming past the same spot I again saw the dog. This time I stopped and approached cautiously. I reached down to pet her and then ran back to town. Instead of changing for a quick shower I found my car keys and drove back to the dog. She was still waiting. I did not find any I.D. tags around her neck. This time I opened the back door to my car and she jumped in. I was never able to locate the owner. "Duchess" became my running partner. She added a lot of joy to the experience. As soon as we got out of town I turned her loose and she ran freely like a pup. Shallow water spots near the road became places for her to skim through. She never tiered of chasing birds.

One of my big regrets in life is that I found it necessary to say goodbye to Duchess. My wife and I decided to move back to the West Coast. We were not sure about our new housing arrangements. We did not know that we would be renting and I assumed that pets would be a problem. A few days before starting out across the country I put Duchess in the car and drove to an animal shelter. As I stooped down to give her a final hug I cried. My tears continued as I drove away, making it hard to see where I was going.

My other canine love affair also ended in tears. A nephew, Richard, gave me a young Boxer/Shepherd pup while I was living in Tacoma, Washington. I built a comfortable doghouse for this second Duchess and fenced off part of the yard as a private dog compound. As Duchess II grew in size she became my constant running companion.

Most of my running was over city streets. Duchess II proved to be a good leash dog. We were a familiar sight in the north-end neighborhoods of Tacoma. Our runs included crossing into park areas where I often unsnapped the lease to give her free run. One day I turned her loose in Point Deviance Park, some five miles from home. We became separated on the wooded trails in the park. When I was ready to turn for home Duchess II was nowhere to be seen. After calling for her, looking around and alerting the park management I decided that my dog was lost and headed back home. As I turned the corner of the block near home I saw Duchess II sitting on the front porch of the house, probably wondering what took me so long!

On another occasion when I turned her loose in a park area closer to the house she also disappeared. I ran home by myself and she returned sometime later forcing a limp leg. I assumed that a car had hit her in her urgency to get back home without me as her escort. Duchess II and I continued to log a lot of hours together on the streets of Tacoma after her injured leg improved.

I lost Duchess II as one of the casualties of divorce. After 45 years of marriage Stella surprised me with divorce papers. This was a very difficult time for me. Two important consolations were that I had my dog and that I could run. In the process of moving out of "our" home a major consideration was finding a rental that would accept a big dog. I did find such a place but it was below the standard of housing I expected. Duchess II seemed to know that I was going through a hard time. She would give me a lick on the face and crawl up at the foot of my bed at night. I ran with her every day. She was a true companion. Unfortunately, I moved to a place where she would not be welcome. This made me go through another traumatic parting as I stooped down to hug another Duchess with tears in my eyes at an Animal Shelter.

As I have shared above, running is always much more than crossing the finish line. There are lots of incidental, not so important, miscellaneous experiences that become part of the package. Like most people, I know that I have often not done a good job of looking after the small stuff of life. It is, of course, much more than the ultimate goal. Years ago I decided to complete a study of running and family life, a reasonable aspiration for a sociologist. I was surprised to find that running was not always a good thing for the family. A runner sometimes became so preoccupied with the running that family life suffered. Wives sometimes said that they were ready to give their spouse an ultimatum: it is either me or the running. The running spouse spent all of his free time either running or going to events. This was in addition to time-consuming commuting to work in a large city like New York. Taking the time for a shared cup of tea, mutual enjoyment of a movie from Netflix, a soft kiss, and other small things become very important in the daily blessing of marriage. Remembering a birthday or an anniversary becomes more important than crossing the finish line of a marathon in some distant city.

One of my marathons in Indiana came at a time of the year when the weather turned bitter cold. Most runners wore cotton gloves and two layers of running gear. Out on the course I fell in step with a younger runner from another state. As we ran together we talked. He always passed a paper cup to me at the Aid stations and at one point reached across my face with a gloved hand to wipe away a flow of spent water. We ran along like two drunks hanging together. Late in the race he took a wrong turn, adding a mile to his run. He caught up with me at the finish line. As we showered in a local High School gym after the run I proclaimed to him and all who wanted to hear that this was my last marathon. I hurt too much. My new friend said simply that he made it a point never to make such a decision immediately after a race. Most of my running came after that intention of voluntary retirement!

Getting off the beaten road to travel the "blue highways" of America has become popular. Details of local life are lost when sitting comfortably in a car traveling 65 or 70 miles an hour on a busy interstate. The best way to really see the land would be to walk. But running is a second best. Committed runners often know more about the flora and fauna of a given location than people who have spent all of their life in a specific locale but have never ventured far from TV and front lawn. I have now run in events from Boston, Massachusetts to Seaside, Oregon. I ran regularly in the Mid-West where the temperature can vary from a wind chill in the winter of 60 degrees below zero to 90 degrees in the summer with 90% humidity.

The winter cold calls for several layers of clothing plus a ski mask over the face and warm gloves. I usually ran on the sidewalk or on the shoulder of the road out of town. Back in Illinois I stopped my regular winter workouts, not because of the cold but because of the potential danger from on-coming cars along a snowy, icy stretch of highway. Weather changes are felt immediately when running in the elements. Lots of little things along a running course change with the weather. In Illinois turtles would sometimes appear on the asphalt road after a heavy rain. I often picked them up, putting them down on the other side of the road to prevent instant turtle soup as a car sped by. My favorite place to run is on the ocean beach along the west coast. The energy of the ebb and flow of mild waters or angry waves, instantaneous changes in the water line and the sight of sea birds all add to the zest of a seaside run. One early morning run at Westport on the Washington Coast gave me a special gift in the form of a large, glass float used in fishing which carried a Japanese imprint. The green glass was partially buried in the sand. I quickly freed this catch from the hard-packed surround and carried it back to my motel room where I gave it a warm bath. Locals told me that floats of this size are very hard to find. One man living near the beach goes out every morning with his pick-up truck guided by a searchlight as he looks for interesting debris left by waters reaching back to distant ports of call. I try to run on the hard-packed sand every time I am able to get to the ocean coast in Washington, Oregon or California.

Running on the sand at the beach or along a busy street gives immediate exposure to the castaway trivia of our culture. Spent plastic in all shapes and colors lies inert beside living miniature sea critters along the ocean beach. City streets become a dumping ground for paper and sometimes aluminum cans or glass bottles. A wet, limp condom lay innocently along the running path as my dog and I made our rounds one afternoon. I have found money, both coins and folded in the form of a $5.00 bill. On two occasions I returned found billfolds to surprised owners. I must admit that I have also stopped to pick a flower or two along the running route, being careful to avoid personal property. These purloined flowers formed a runner's bouquet carried for miles back home to my wife.

The Boston Marathon merits more attention than the simple statement that I finished the course twice. My most difficult running came while I was running with a friend who also wanted to do the Boston. Since he was under 40 he needed a sub three-hour qualifying run. As I trained with him we decided to enter a marathon in Michigan that offered a fairly flat course for his pre-Boston run. He was pushing 6 and ½ minutes at times. I kept up with him for about 16 miles. At that point I was completely exhausted. I stopped running and pulled out of the race. When I did I looked behind me at the runners coming my way. They truly looked like "warmed over death" and I wondered for the first time what I looked like late in a race. This was the only marathon I failed to finish after starting.

My most memorable marathon prior to my first Boston was the event at Whitewater, Wisconsin. At that time my son, Steven, had just completed his driving exam. He was my back-up support, driving the car over the length of the course. The Whitewater event began and ended at a college campus. The course wound through farm country. At near the 20-mile mark some of the young runners began sharing jokes, a form of tension release. One runner asked his partner; "What do you have when you have wall-to-wall cows in a barn?" The answer, "udder confusion!" Another runner began singing; "I'm strong to the finish because I eat my spinach...I'm Popeye the sailor man." The need to urinate wasn't a major problem for the men but one of the women sought our advice about what she should do for a bathroom break. One suggestion was that she knock on the door of a farm hose, another was that she might hide behind some rows of corn. As I approached the finish area a college-aged student pointed in the right direction with the greeting of "sir." I did not appreciate the word. For me "sir" is associated with someone who is older as well as superior. I felt that I had earned the right to be regarded as just one of the runners.

Since I was living in Indianapolis at the time of my first Boston I managed to arrange a ride with a high school teacher in Kokomo and one of his students. I reserved a room in the YMCA in Boston. Two weeks before this event I developed a serious problem around my right big toe which necessitated surgical attention. I could not run for two weeks. In my room at the Y the night before the race I pondered what to do about my toe. I decided to cut off part of my stocking to allow for more room. I was able to run the event.

I was surprised by the crowd of runners milling around the starting area out at Hopington. Runners lined up on the street according to their qualifying time. It took me six minutes to get up to the starting line when the gun went off. One runner in line in front of me started off bare-footed. He had trained without shoes. He attracted the attention of the media. Another young runner also drew special attention. He was one of my students at IUPUI. I knew that his dream was to do the Boston. I also knew that he had survived a 1,000-foot free-fall when his chute failed him while he was performing in a special parachute team at a county fair. He broke 17 bones in the fall but fell into some shrubs at the home of a doctor who was present at the time. This doctor immediately took him into an ER. This young man had extensive surgery and then a long time of rehab. He first took long walks, then was able to jog and finally to run at a slow pace. He never completed a qualifying marathon before the Boston. He never had an official number. But running near the back of the crowd, he did complete the distance and was mentioned in a national magazine.

At Boston people living in the area lined the course. Many held a local paper that included a listing of all runners with numbers and names. It was very encouraging to hear your name called out as you ran along. After some 10 miles into the race I was running along with a small group of four others. One of the group had penned his number to an outer jacket. As it turned warmer he wanted to remove this jacket. We formed a team to help him take off the jacket and pin his number to an inside T shirt. One of us held the safety pins. Another held the jacket and then we reversed this process. As I ran up Heartbreak Hill one of the spectators standing along the street who held a portable radio announced that Will Rogers had just crossed the finish line. I find it hard to comprehend how the world class runners can sustain the speed they do over 26 miles. At the Prudential Building the race came to an abrupt end at the finish area. There was no free space to ease into a standing position. I was just glad to finish the distance, a major accomplishment for me.

Now it is time to move away from running as I continue my story of walking the streets of downtown late at night. The next chapter shares some of the events that unfolded as I worked to start a night ministry in Portland, Oregon. Since I did this while holding a position at the University of Washington my work at that time was primarily only on the week-end and as a volunteer.

Chapter 3

Walking the Streets at Night in the City of Roses; Portland, Oregon

Lessons from Three Hotels

The Estate Hotel:

As I started commuting from Seattle to Portland to start a program of Operation Nightwatch for that city in 1979 one of my first goals was to learn more about the people who lived or spent some of the night around Burnside downtown. To enhance my education, I decided to stay in the old Estate Hotel on two occasions. This hotel, near Burnside, had deteriorated considerably over the years. I paid $4.00 a night for my room, plus $1.00 for a key deposit. When I unlocked the door to my room and turned on the light an army of cockroaches scrambled up one wall in disarray, fleeing from any possible harm from the light that glowed from a single bulb hanging from a cord in the center of the room. This was something of an enigma because the room was really well suited for cockroaches, not for creatures standing tall on two legs. There was a single bed and a few blankets and one wooden chair, nothing more. A common bathroom was down the hall. The window was bare, with no kind of curtain. I draped some of my extra clothes over this window before climbing into bed. I also forced the chair up against the door knob as an added precaution after locking it. I heard that a man had been shot through the door of one of these rooms.

This was a place for cockroaches. I should have been the one hurrying away from the room. I was familiar with the normal comforts of home and family, a living room with amenities such as a soft, comfortable couch and the always present TV. Cockroaches needed no amenities. This "hotel" room stood in stark contrast to places where I stayed when presenting papers at national meetings of the American Sociological Association. During one meeting in New York I stayed at the Hilton Hotel. I also stayed in the best hotels in other cities such as New Orleans and San Francisco. I had an academic position at a leading university; I had a PhD in sociology. Why was I staying at the Estate Hotel off Burnside in downtown Portland? The appeal of this old hotel was what it might offer in helping me better understand the people I wanted to serve.

The men who were staying in the Estate Hotel at that time had very few amenities inside the hotel to give them some kind of diversion at night. But most stayed inside, apprehensive about possible danger on the streets at night. One night, not far from the hotel, three men attacked an older man. They found nothing of value in his pockets but did notice a shine coming from his mouth. So they proceeded to knock him to the ground and then forced dental work from his mouth, hoping to get at least a little silver or gold.

From personal experience I was aware of violence on the streets at night. One night around midnight I was walking toward Marlina's tavern not far from Burnside when I noticed an emergency vehicle parked at the curb. Technicians were loading something into the back of this vehicle. They were in no hurry as they lifted the body of Big John, a regular at Marlina's. I heard the details of this death when I talked to Marlina in her tavern. Big John was nearing the door to her place when three young men jumped from a passing car and surrounded him with knives in their hands. They killed Big John and then sped away before the police came. I never learned the reasons for this attack. My role that night was to give some words of comfort to Marlina. She became a strong supporter of my program of night ministry, serving on the Board of Directors for a time.

Back in my room at the Estate Hotel I found a man headed down the hall for his room which was next to mine. I watched as he staggered toward his door and then struggled in a drunken haze to unlock the door. I helped him access his room and then directed him to his bed where he collapsed.

One major take-home lesson from my first stay in the Estate was that people who stay in very inadequate housing or remain on the street all night can be very lonely. I found that there was no one to talk to. I was all alone. Social interaction is important for everyone. It is very difficult to sustain interaction with nothing to offer in the process of social exchange. In normal circumstances, for example, if someone buys you a cup of coffee you would return the favor. But if you have no money this is not possible. This holds true in the church community as well. Small group gatherings in the homes of members can become a showcase for displaying a large house and/or very expensive items to eat and or drink. People in a church have value in and of themselves, regardless of where they live or how much money they have. When writing about suicide I did some reading on the cases of people jumping off the Golden Gate Bridge. A few people have survived this fatal plunge. When one man died his personal belongings were found which included a diary. His final note was that he would not take the plunge to death if one person stopped him on the way to the bridge with a smile or a word of welcome. Obviously this did not happen and he jumped to his death. It is important to interact with others. This must be encouraged in the church and in every setting where people gather.

During my second and final stay at the Estate Hotel I came away with new impressions. I was given a different room this time. This room did have a small sink but no mirror over the sink. One of the hotel employees loaned me a piece of broken, discarded mirror. The cockroaches in this second room where a sight to behold. When I lifted a wash cloth near the sink they were everywhere.

I was recovering from a viral infection on this second visit to the Estate. Late at night as I lay on my bed in the small room I heard a man coughing down the hall. This was a very deep cough. Since I had just gone through a sick spell during which I had the normal attention of family members, I wondered what it would be like to be sick and all alone. How does a person cope in a situation where there is no one to go for cough syrup, no money for cough syrup and no one to show an interest in your condition? Health and health care are major problems for the poor. At the Estate the residents seldom got out of the building. An alcoholic in such a situation would depend on a barter system to get alcohol up the stairs. Any kind of monthly check would soon be completely spent in such a situation.

As you might imagine, there were many ways in which my activities changed during my limited stay at the Estate. There was nothing in the bare room to interest me. I had a practice of relaxing at night by watching TV news and network shows. But this room had no TV or radio. I found myself going out on the street much earlier than was my custom in night ministry. On my last Saturday in this place I awoke before 7AM and started getting ready for a new day. I had a morning meeting to attend, a bus to catch for my return to Seattle and things to do upon my return home. As I was dressing and packing my cheap suitcase I was suddenly impressed by the silence around me. No one else was getting ready for the day. These men had little to get ready for. One of the major deprivations of the poor, I realized, is not having something meaningful to do.

The Holme Hotel:

Another hotel in town offered me more free lessons on what it can be like when someone ends up with late-stage alcoholism. One night I met Tom on the street in Portland and he wanted to talk. His clothes and speech were tattered. His right arm was wrapped around a brown paper sack holding something bottle shaped. I was familiar with his fraternity, a close-knit society of men and women dedicated primarily to the pursuit of their next drink. This man wanted to show me where he was living.

I climbed steep stairs off the street with my new friend to step inside the labyrinth of disorder that was the Holme Hotel. As I climbed the stairs I thought about the men who were regulars on these stairs and the dues they paid to be in this place. This was a turf given to the idiosyncrasies of serious alcoholics. The membership dues were heavy; hearing the harsh rebuke of a wife or other family member, sometimes for years; feeling the gut wrenching pain of withdrawal when no alcohol was available; the ready image of friends who were "successful" with jobs, homes and leisure activities. Near the top of the stairs I heard a man trying to share a recent sight on the street below. As he spoke in words slurred by alcohol he was trying to describe his unexpected sighting of a VW bug "the size and shape of a pink elephant."

Tom showed me his room. It was more like a small space for the collection of junk than a living space. His small, single bed was covered with a loose pile of blankets. Empty beer cans were the most prominent decoration for this room. The ceiling was not softly painted plaster or sheet rock. It was cheap chicken wire.

Out in the common area in front of a space controlled by the official in charge, the "clerk" I noticed an odd assortment of empty cough syrup bottles. This reminded me that when pressed an alcoholic will grab anything that contains even the limited hope of a little alcohol. The floor of this room was not bereft of adornment. In places I noted what appeared to be brown clumps of human feces. It appeared that for some men the long run of 20 or 30 feet to the bathroom was just too much to handle.

One of my strongest memories related to the Holme Hotel is a visit in connection with helping a man, Andrew, as he struggled with profound paranoia. For him the sky was truly falling, pointedly and determinedly directly on him. I met this man when I dropped into an emergency shelter on Burnside Street. When he saw my clergy collar he immediately came over to stand by me. He was very anxious as he explained that snakes were coming out of the empty cup he was holding. He informed me, confidentially, that FBI agents were after him. This man was very serious about his paranoid delusions. It would have been futile to have attempted a direct attack on his images. I listened and wondered why he trusted me.

Andrew asked if he could walk around with me all night. I told him that I would not be out all night but invited him to leave the shelter with me as I headed west on Burnside Street back to downtown Portland. As we walked along in the dark I learned a little more about my new friend. He was not unfamiliar with institutional care and expressed a desire to see a professional that night. I knew that the University of Oregon hospital system accepted mentally ill patients for screening if they appeared in person in the emergency room. I did not know how I could get this man to the hospital, located some distance up a hill from the downtown area. I did not have a car in town. I had taken the bus down from Seattle for the weekend.

I did have $10 in cash as my total reserve to cover my expenses the rest of the night plus any needs as I rode the bus early in the morning for my trip back to Seattle. This would be a four-hour bus trip for me. I signaled a passing cab and asked the driver what he would charge to take my friend up to the hospital. He said that he could make the trip for $5. I held the back door of the cab open for Andrew and wished him well as I handed $5 to the cab driver.

I had a sense of minor accomplishment but also a feeling of uneasiness about my friend as I walked away from the cab. For some reason I decided to pay a visit to the Holme Hotel before calling it a night. I went there not because of the filth and the agony of alcoholism but because I had on occasion chatted with one of the clerks on duty and felt that he enjoyed my presence. During other visits I talked with him about his trips to Alaska in former years and about his aunt who was a missionary. On this particular night the clerk I knew was on duty. It was a few days before Christmas. He surprised me by announcing that he had a Christmas present for me. He left the desk, went to his room and then came back with his gift, handing it to me with a smile. I was totally surprised as I opened the package to find a small pocket flashlight wrapped in a $10 bill! How could such a gift come from a place like the Holme? I spent $5 on a stranger and was given $10 by someone else, all within 45 minutes!

The Governor Hotel:

I was invited to speak to the local Rotary Club, meeting in the Governor Hotel. At that time this was one of the largest Rotary Clubs in the country. My appearance in the main ballroom of the Governor came in stark contrast to life as I saw it near Burnside that day or during the hours of the evening. On my way to the Governor I watched as men eagerly searched downtown dumpsters for any scrap of food they could find. This "dumpster diving" was another world away from the scene that was spread out before me at the Rotary luncheon meeting. I sat on an elevated stage, looking out at a crowd of well fed and well-dressed men, some of the local leaders in Portland.

After my talk one of the Rotary Club members invited me to join him in his private club the next day for lunch. At his club I was treated to a place at a table covered with a white, linen table cloth. I stared at the large assortment of tableware, not sure which fork or spoon I should use first. I decided on the chicken pot pie. In my experience this meat dish was inclined to be on the soggy side. It seemed like a safe bet for me to tackle without making a scene. But when I speared the crust of this gourmet dish crumbs flew over the table. In contrast to the frozen pies I was used to, this dish had been freshly baked and it was very flaky.

My new Rotary friend proceeded to explain why he had invited me to lunch. It turned out that he was a self-made millionaire. He owned a business block in downtown Portland which was the nesting place for a high-rise commercial building. But he told me that he had "come up from the bottom." Years before our meeting he had been down and out. This made him interested in my work at night. He did not, however, make a major financial contribution to the work of Nightwatch in Portland. It was not unusual to find people drawn to the program because of their own experiences. One downtown Portland pastor, for example, was interested in helping my work primarily because he had experienced poverty himself.

Important People in Downtown Portland

General Dwight D. Eisenhower:

I did not see General and then President Eisenhower on the streets around Burnside at night. But I want to use him as a point of reference. I happened to be on a downtown Portland street in 1952 when he was riding through the city in an open convertible during his campaign for President. Streets were closed off. Crowds gathered on the sidewalks. This military and then political leader was given a lot of attention. From my present vantage point I am thinking about what makes anyone "special" or important. Not many of us ride into town in a motor caravan with streets packed with well-wishers. But we share a lot with those who are "famous." Like them, all of us live a limited period of time. We all face death. Also, all of us are truly important. We may not receive national attention but we have value, we are all important.

Meeting under an umbrella:

In 1980 I felt good about my running accomplishments. I was not a nationally known leader of men. But a number of things gave me a feeling of worth. In addition to my running exploits, I held a faculty position at the University of Washington. The work on the dark side of downtown Portland came on the week-ends. What a contrast between my personal life and the condition of those I saw around Burnside in Portland at night!

One rainy, dark night as I walked the downtown streets of Portland I was carrying a large, black umbrella. Tom, a man in his early 20's came up to me to beg for a cigarette. When he saw my clergy collar he changed his request into a plea for a listening ear. Together we walked over to the protective covering of a building entrance that offered some relief from the torrents of rain. This commercial space had closed for business hours before.

Tom first wanted me to know that he was out of the hospital "against medical advice." He pulled a loose-fitting shirt back away from his right shoulder to display deep scars. I was told that he had undergone many surgical procedures for bone cancer. They wanted him to stay in the hospital. But he walked away. Cancer was only one of the many heavy concerns hounding Tom. One of his most painful memoires involved the loss of his wife and small child. There was an automobile accident. Tom was driving the car. Both his wife and child were killed. He could not understand why he wasn't taken with them. "I should have died...I am going to die" was his mantra, repeated over and over as he wept openly. He also told me that he was "no good, worth nothing."

After sharing in his trauma around the death of family members, I was invited to journey back in time with Tom to Vietnam. He then went into another tirade about the times of killing while he was in the service. For him these killings were a personal affair for which he felt guilt. To add to his problems, Tom was an alcoholic. That night he said that he was on "downers." Then he freely admitted that he was on his way to make a delivery of illegal drugs. Tom showed no interest in living. For him the future held only the possibility of death.

When it became my turn to respond to this litany of pain and guilt I said something like "I assume that you want some response from me as a minister. Do you want me to pray with you?" When Tom replied in the affirmative I invited him to gather up all of his agony and then to hold it up to God. As I placed a hand on his shoulder I closed my eyes and began to pray. After only a few words Tom stopped me to say "there's something else, I've killed a man." I instructed him to add this to the list of things and to hold it all up to God. As we prayed, Tom reached out once to gently hold me back away from the rain that was falling just beyond the reach of the protective overhang of the building. As we parted he reached into a pocket to give me all of his money. I refused the money, informing him that my reward was in serving as a minister to the folks on the street at night.

I find it hard to share these life experiences with folks I saw at night. As I write this I am sitting in a warm room at the University of Colorado in Boulder. I have just finished my hot tea from my thermos and I am eating cookies prepared for me by my wife, Ruth. At noon I will eat the lunch she has prepared for me. It is Valentine's Day and I can see that the lunch includes a lovely, heart-shaped box of chocolates, a surprise for me. It is 20 degrees outside and snow is forecast for this afternoon in February. But I have warm clothes and I will be walking from one heated building to another. The people I saw at night had very little going for them. They often faced each day with a deep sense of personal failure.

"I'm no good"

Some nights in Portland I walked east on the Burnside Street Bridge away from the downtown area to talk with people hanging around an emergency shelter. One night in that part of town I was pulled into a conversation with Paul, a man in his mid-50's. He seemed very anxious. That day he had looked for work. For a dishwashing job or anything. But he found nothing. The only thing he had to show for his efforts was a painful display of blisters on both feet. As I talked with Paul another man came along and sat down beside us. This other man was several years older than Paul. At the sight of this third person Paul spoke again of his plight including his view of his own worth. He informed me that he was… "no g. d. good, no good for nothing." Then he turned to the older man, pointed a finger at him and said "that guy gets a Social Security check, he is worth something. I ain't worth nothing to nobody." This estimation of self-worth is one of the most devastating aspects of chronic unemployment or underemployment. I tried to assure Paul that he did have value, that he was important.

Dean C. Jones

"Bless me"

I am in debt to Portland for giving me one of the most memorable experiences of my 20 years of doing night ministry. Late one day I met three men on a sidewalk near Burnside. They were carrying well-used back-packs and wearing clothes that had not seen a washer or dryer in some time. All three had recently arrived in town but they were not greeted by a welcome wagon. Their arrival came after a very long ride over the rails in an empty box-car. After climbing up into this box-car in St. Louis they had no control over their destiny. The doors were open to all kinds of weather. They bounced in unison with every jarring move of the car on rails. When these men saw me they first asked where they might get something to eat. I directed them to the local mission.

Later as darkness fell over the city I saw these three men again. One of them pulled away from his buddies, looked at me, and said "I need to talk." We walked ahead of the others and stopped near a parking meter on the sidewalk. Then the railroad man turned to me with a request. "Bless me" was his plea as he looked at my clergy collar. I extended one arm to place it on his shoulder, closed my eyes and prayed for him. When I opened my eyes after this prayer I saw a face that was radiant, transformed. Something very real happened that night. I walked away from the man feeling like I was walking on a cloud. Looking back, I wonder why one of the most intense spiritual events for me happened in the dark, along a sidewalk downtown instead of under the bright lights of a church sanctuary during a regular hour of worship.

A bartender in potential danger:

Not all encounters at night were that dramatic. Sometimes a very simple act was needed. One night, for example, I sat at the bar drinking a diet Coke in a small tavern off Burnside. It was after 1 AM. The bar would close at 2 AM. A woman was tending bar, the only employee present. Three men walked in and immediately started being very obnoxious. One slammed an ashtray down on the bar, sending ashes scattering. The men were loud and very offensive as they spoke to the bartender. I felt that I should simply remain in this place until closing time to give the bartender some support. So I sat as the minutes ticked by until the three men left.

A woman "of the night:"

Another night I was sitting on a bar stool in another night spot when a woman came over to take the empty stool on my left. She started asking questions like… "how long you going to be in town?" Her talk identified her as one of the "women of the night," a prostitute. She was thinking that I was a business man in town, maybe looking for some "action." When I deliberately turned to face her and in the process displayed my white clergy collar the conversation changed immediately. She wanted to talk about her children and her family so I listened.

This encounter reminds me of some of the encounters one of my clergy volunteers reported years later when I was working in Tacoma, Washington. This volunteer seemed to be especially called to talk to the young, male prostitutes who loitered around a particular intersection downtown. He too reported long conversations about family. This was something the young men needed to talk about but not something that would be discussed in their chance encounters with potential customers.

A man hiding under a bed:

One night I met a man on Burnside who was obviously someone who was familiar with the city's mental health system. I talked with him and he told me where he was staying. The next time I was in that part of town at night I did not see him around so I decided to try to find him at the address he had given me. When I climbed a flight of stairs and knocked on his door there was no response. Seeing that the door was not locked I walked into the small room. I did not see anyone immediately. Then I noticed a shoe sticking out from under a bed. Looking closer, I found the man crawled up under his bed. I contacted the mental health emergency number, suggesting that this man most likely needed to be in a special facility.

Around Lake Tahoe the Hard Way

One of my concerns in Portland was how to generate funds for the newly forming program. I filed for non-profit, 501(C) (3) status, gathered together a Board of Directors and was able to recruit some local clergy volunteers. I also spoke in churches and to service clubs including Rotary and Kiwanis when given the opportunity. Once I was featured in the local paper and I had an appearance on a local TV show.

I became creative in raising funds for the program. Since I was addicted to long distance running I decided to use this as a way to obtain funding. I heard that Pepsi of Reno was sponsoring a 72 mile run around Lake Tahoe so I started spreading the word that I would run this event, asking for pledges of so much per mile. I was familiar with the 26.2-mile marathon distance and runs of 50 miles, but never a 72 miler. Looking back, I do not understand how I was able to train for the run around Lake Tahoe. The daily work-outs of 10 miles could be worked into my schedule. But I also needed a long run every week. Since I was living in Seattle I decided to run around Green Lake. Running 12 times around this lake for a long work-out took a lot of time. I was working at the time and commuting to Portland to work the night scene. I did not keep a diary. I do not see how I had the time to train and then to make the trip to Reno for the event. But I did all of this and raised about $1,000 for the fledgling program of Operation Nightwatch, Portland.

The day before the run my wife, Stella and I drove to South Tahoe where we found a Motel 6 for the night. Early in the morning on the day of the run we drove to the starting line on the California side of the lake. At the dawn of a new day with the new sun inviting people to the casinos or other places of fun my focus was on the immediate surface along the shoulder of the road as I ran along with other men and women. As I ran I was surprised to see that some had adopted a run-walk strategy. As I had no experience with anything over 50 miles I did not know how to proceed. I simply kept the pace I knew for a 50 miler.

Lake Tahoe is a very scenic lake, even from a limited view while running. As I ran on the road in California, headed for the south end of the lake, I started focusing on my legs, sending them messages to keep up the good work. This was prompted by comments from my daughter, Kathy, who was introduced to bio-feedback in a psychology class she was taking at the time. At about 45 miles I was running in Nevada with my number pinned to a T shirt as I passed a small commercial area where people were walking from shops to their cars. One man among the shoppers had a question for me.

"What's going on," He asked as he pointed to the runners ahead of me. I told him that they were running around the lake but that I probably would not make it. My wife was parked just off the road near the 50-mile point. I made my way to the car and stretched out for a few minutes in the back seat. Then I told her that I needed to see her "every mile" and got out of the car to start running again.

With my ever-present water bottle and a bottle of Gater Aid I continued on the course. At one point I pleaded with my wife to get me a milk shake. She tried but was unsuccessful in finding a store nearby. The group of runners at the beginning of the run gradually thinned out. At around 50 miles I was running alone. Near the 60 mile point I started walking and walked for 6 or 7 miles before starting to run again. By then it was starting to get dark and I began to worry about finding the finish line. Then a younger runner caught up with me. He knew the way to the finish line. As we ran along together we talked about who should cross the finish line first. He said that I should go ahead of him because I was older. I told him that I would let him cross before me because he was younger. As we neared the small crowd hanging around the finish line we locked arms and ran across together. I was very emotional, crying out for my wife. She was not immediately around. A woman who was a stranger to me came over and gave me a hug. When Stella appeared she drove us to a small restaurant where she ordered a pizza. I drank cold water and a soft drink but could not handle food. I did sleep well that night and a few days later I was out running again.

In the pages of the next chapter I invite you to follow me to Denver and St. Louis and then to Tacoma, Washington. I decided not to continue with my work in Portland. The program in Portland was modeled and named after Operation Nightwatch in Seattle.

Operation Nightwatch in Portland - Update

The work I started in Portland has now been serving the homeless and needy of the city for over 30 years. Today the story, in print and colorful pictures, is shared on a web site and in a monthly newsletter. The mailing address is: P.O. Box 4005, Portland, OR, 97208. The office is located at: 1432 S.W. 11th Ave. in Portland. The telephone number is: (503) 220-0438. The Director, Gary Davis, can be reached at: exec@operationnightwatch.org. As I have shared, the

Dean C. Jones

first full-time Director of this program was Gary Vaughan. He worked with volunteers as they served the homeless in doorways, loading docks and campsites in downtown Portland. In time a Hospitality Center was established. Here the homeless and other low-income people could gather with others for the evening, socializing, sharing stories as well as coffee and sandwiches. This center is now the hub of Nightwatch with foot care clinics, monthly Birthday Nights and Comedy Movie Nights. This is also a place where people can get blankets, clothing and personal hygiene items at a time when no other helping agencies are open.

The second Executive Director, Debbie Coppenger, did much to set Nightwatch on a stable institutional and fiscal footing.

The Current Executive Director, Gary Davis, expanded the program to include Street Hospitality Teams. These well-trained crews connect directly with people who cannot or will not access the Hospitality Center itself. He also started the Mobile Hospitality Center, enabling Nightwatch to expand the work to homeless clusters located outside the immediate downtown core.

Chapter 4

In The Mile-High City:
Living, Running and Night Ministry
In Denver, Colorado

Lookout Mountain, Guanella Pass, the Past and Running

Two large stone pillars welcome all at the base of Lookout Mountain just out of Golden, Colorado. The silent message is: "bring me your dreams; the clean, high-altitude air of the mountain will sustain you." Through the years, including the years when I lived far from Denver, I always looked forward to a run up this mountain when I visited in Colorado. My last trip up and down this elevated monument to Buffalo Bill was a jog four years ago when I was 79. From the mountain-focused eyes of a true Coloradan, Lookout is not really a "mountain." It is really only a "foothill" standing a mere 7,374 feet in altitude. Not a match for the majestic 14,000 footers in the Rocky Mountain chain.

Running is not a significant part of the legacy of this mountain. As I have indicated, I was born in Denver in 1932. My family moved to Seattle when I was seven. Lookout Mountain is best known as the final resting place of Buffalo Bill Cody. His gravesite shares the top of Lookout with a restaurant, museum and gift shop. At different places in a ride or run up Lookout some truly spectacular views east of downtown Denver are offered free of charge. Buffalo Bill was born in Scott County Iowa in 1846. He died in Denver in 1917. There were many highpoints in his life. He rode in the pony express, fought in the Civil War and was a prospector in the Pike's Peak gold rush of 1859. But he became most famous for his touring Wild West show. This captured attention in part because of his fame in facing the buffalo. He killed over 4,000 buffalo.

Over the years many have followed the curving mountain road up to the top of Lookout. My father talked about one of his ways to make some money when he was a child back in the 1920's. He was forced to become creative. In one of his schemes, he set up a water stand at the base of Lookout Mountain. Back then cars were not blessed with the efficient cooling systems of today. He gave drivers water before they climbed the hill for a small charge. Money was always a problem in the family. My paternal grandfather, George Jones, talked about making money from moonshiners as he stood at the base of the mountain, ready to warn those making illegal booze if he saw federal agents approaching.

Lookout Mountain has life lessons for those who will stop to look and listen. The road up does not go straight up. Like all mountain roads, it has switchbacks, and curves. Life also has switchbacks and curves. It is not a straight, linear line to ultimate "success." There are detours, challenges and even dead-ends. Sometimes the only way to proceed forward is to back out and try another route. When I ran up and down Lookout I always saw the steel frame of what was once a car. Far down a steep canyon, it was only a broken pile of rusted and weathering steel. Once it had known better days, times of carrying happy families for outings in the summer and joyful excursions to work and other places. In my work of ministry, I have often been asked to say the formal words at a funeral or memorial service. Sometimes the end of earthly life comes as a tragedy, something like falling off a high cliff. Other times the end comes as the slow result of the gradual erosion of the stuff of life.

Another reality of life that was very evident on Lookout was that there are much easier ways to travel than running along the shoulder of a road. At one place on the Mountain there is space for a few cars to pull off. This was used by people who were into hang gliding. They parked, unloaded their equipment including the soft arms of an abbreviated parachute with its comfortable harness eager to transport a man or woman safely and slowly over the road and down the mountain to a waiting landing area. Gliding through the warm air does not require much physical excretion. Nothing like a run or jog up Lookout. For those who are not into hang gliding the most popular way to get from one place to another is to drive, again requiring only the ability to sit and to know something about how to navigate a car.

Looking back at my many ascents of Lookout Mountain, I cannot recall a time when others were on the shoulder of the road. It was always a solo experience. That was not the case when I moved to Denver from Seattle to start a night ministry program for the city in 1984 and decided to do a competitive run from Georgetown up to Guanella Pass and then a 50-mile event in downtown Denver. Guanella Pass rises to an elevation of 11,669 feet. The start in Georgetown gave runners the advantage of beginning at an altitude of 8,530 feet. As I stood with other runners in a park waiting for the race to begin we were joined by a young runner who said that he had parked his car up at the Pass and run down to join us! Not exactly a smart thing to do! As with other runs in Colorado I was impressed by the view from up at the top of Guanella Pass. A major memory of this event is that my daughter, Kathy, drove up to the top to give me a ride back down.

Family memories also surround this running event for me. Back in the late 1930's my maternal grandfather, Charles Houchens, spent one winter near Georgetown in a cabin as he re-worked a silver mine. This was a common practice. When a mine was no longer profitable for a regular commercial operation it was simply passed on to a freelance miner who worked, looking for any possible remnants in the already worked parcel of ground. As a child of six I remember going down a short distance into a large hole in the ground as my grandfather explained what he did. I can also recall seeing a herd of wild horses in a meadow close to his cabin. I do not see how anyone could survive the social isolation of a winter in a cabin up in the mountains. Of course there was no TV, no radio, no cell phone, and no telephone. He did make infrequent trips into Georgetown for supplies. As I recall he talked about the sounds of bear outside the locked door of his living space.

Recently a regular marathon has attracted runners along Colfax in Denver. But I have not heard anything recently about a 50 miler in Denver. Back in 1984 there was such an event. We ran over Denver streets and along Cherry Creek early in the spring when there was still snow on the ground. One of my memories of this event is that for the first time in my running career I started out beside a man who was "running" the course in a wheeled gurney. He did not have the free use of his legs. He looked up at me with a greeting and a smile. When I saw him again at about the 10 mile point he again smiled and I smiled back. But late in the course I simply did not have the energy to return his greeting. After this race we met in the home of the race organizer. I was given a plaque for being the first in my age category but this plaque does not have a time on it.

Pikes Peak or bust:

The phrase "Pikes Peak or Bust" was the slogan of the Colorado Gold Rush. At one time lots of people came to the state in a flurry of excitement about striking it rich in silver or gold. At an altitude of 14, 115 feet the Peak stands high, reaching for the sky. Unlike the vagaries of life on the street at night the Colorado Mountains offer a sense of stability. They stand tall through the onslaught of cold and snow in the winter, the changing colors of fall and the fresh new growth in the spring. They never become discouraged about status in terms of work position. They have offered new hope and inspiration for people over the years.

As a National Historic Landmark, Pikes Peak has known many very special events. For example, in 1893 Katharine Lee Bates was so inspired by the view from the top that she penned the lines for the famous national song, "America the Beautiful." There is a gift shop and restaurant at the summit. The most popular ways to reach the top are to drive up an asphalt road, to take a ride on the cog railroad or to walk up the Barr Trail. In 1913 William Brown drove the 20 miles to the summit in 5 hours and 28 minutes. More recently a car race has been part of the Pikes Peak scene. In 2012 Fumo Nutahara, driving an electric Toyota, covered the same distance in 10 minutes and 15 seconds. In 1984 two foot races used the Barr Trail, starting at the trail head just past the cog railroad depot in Manitou Springs. One race, on Saturday, was an ascent of the Peak. Then on Sunday there was a run that went up the mountain and then back down the same trail. I decided to do the ascent only, over the organic trail of dirt and gravel compared to the asphalt covered road for cars.

Going up the Peak on the trail, either walking or running, offers spectacular views not available to a race car driver. I can remember the view from the first few switchbacks along the trail as I ran along with others. Running was possible during the first part of the 8,000 feet in elevation gain on the way up the 13-mile trail. There was also a fairly flat part of the trail at mid-mountain where running was a possibility. In this mid-mountain interlude, I was running with a few others when one of them pointed ahead to a man running alone. His comment was … "That guy will win – he runs to work every morning and he works up at the top." Not a possibility, of course. But it did introduce some levity into the arduous run. Above timberline there was no running. We walked up to the top where we were offered oxygen. I did not need any. Along the open trail above timberline I passed younger runners who had paused to rest on some rocks. It made me feel good in being able to pass them. I drove to Manitou Springs by myself. We were given a free bus ride back to our cars once we reached the top. Like the time of being unemployed, I again went through an event that was significant for me but did it all alone.

From Mountain Vistas to the Hard Sidewalk of Downtown at Night

A frail, elderly woman:

After moving to Denver when I decided not to become involved full time in Portland, Oregon I had many encounters with people as I again walked the downtown streets, wanting to start another Operation Nighwatch program. One person I saw was a frail, elderly woman. In my mind's eye I can still see her today, face weathered and hands worn with age. I often saw her along Larimer Street late at night. I never saw her when she was sober. Her standard posture was to stand or move slowly with head bowed toward the street. For her there were no mountains, no long-range views of enchanting places. And no close family to lean on. She was old and she was an alcoholic. One night as I stood close to her she managed to hang onto the fender and then the hood of a car parked along the street so that she stood tall enough to look me in the eye. Then she put a trembling hand inside her coat pocket to extract a dollar bill. She extended this dollar with hand shaking toward me. I pushed her hand back and told her that she needed to keep the money. Then she rebuked me with the admonition "you mean that I am not good enough to give to God?" I told her that she was certainly worthy, took the dollar and thanked her.

"Why did God do that to my brother:"

There is no way to fully understand life far from ski resorts in the mountains and high-rise lofts in downtown Denver. It is so much more than physical appearance or a litany of what is lacking in the material artifacts that are often taken for granted. The gut-level pain of another is always difficult to measure. As an example, one night I met a man in his mid-60's on the Larimer scene. He had a full, white beard and wore a plaid jacket. When Stan noticed my clergy collar he immediately pulled a small New Testament out of an inside jacket pocked. Next he reached into another pocket and pulled out a large leather sheath holding a sharp knife. After displaying and then carefully replacing these objects, Stan walked with me along the dark sidewalk away from one of the taverns.

As we walked and talked Stan first tried to impress me with a strong macho image. He said that he had made $25 that day while panhandling uptown. He talked about doing 10 years in prison. This was hard time for murder. As he explained it, he actually killed three men, two while in the service and one on the street. Before too long this strong macho image began to fade. Stan seemed to need to share some very deep feelings about his brother. This brother, his hero, gave years of his life in service as the Director of a Mission in Portland, Oregon. But unfortunately this brother developed a severe case of diabetes and then underwent surgery during which both legs were amputated. This became an obsession with Stan. He just could not see how a God of Love could do such a thing to his brother.

The sharing about his brother brought tears to Stan's eyes. He admitted to having frequent episodes of crying himself to sleep beside railroad tracks in strange cities. When sleep came he was often tormented by nightmares. Visions of a final judgment scene dominated these nightmares. He saw himself standing before a large book. An angel looked carefully for his name in the book but never found it. Stan hated God but could not stand the thought of an eternity without God. That night on a downtown street corner at the end of our meeting I placed a hand on Stan's shoulder and prayed as cars passed on the near-by street.

Walking with Violence

In the first chapter I shared a number of stories from the mass media on violence in our contemporary world. As I indicated, some form of violence was never far from my personal journey in downtown, late-night ministry. I also talked with some people apart from my work at night when violence became an important consideration.

. When I was writing a book about the mentally ill offender[2] I talked with a man who was being held in the maximum security unit of a state hospital after he was indicted for shooting and killing a man. He described the killing for me in detail. He said that he was on a downtown sidewalk with a few other people. At the time he thought that he was the apostle Paul. The others were his followers. When he saw a young woman approaching he knew that she was the Virgin Mary. A man put his hand on Mary's shoulder. The man I talked to said that he had a gun at the time. He responded to what he saw as a threat to Virgin Mary. He pulled out his gun and shot the stranger. He really expected people to come down from near-by apartments to congratulate him. Mental illness remains as a major consideration in cases of the most extreme violence.

When I was trying to start a program of night ministry in Aberdeen, Washington I became aware that domestic violence was on the increase after the area fell upon hard times following a decline in the timber industry. Some of the women I saw shared stories of how they were forced to strike out on their own, after their husband became abusive. This was after he was laid off and no longer able to make the daily trips in his pick-up truck out to do manly work among trees.

Late one day in the Aberdeen area I stopped at a small restaurant for a bite to eat. The young woman who served me wanted to talk. She told me about a rare experience. Sometime before our meeting she said that a man, a stranger to her, came in and ordered a meal. Then he left a $5 tip. At that time this was a very big tip. Later in the day, as they were closing, this same man came back and offered her a ride home. She accepted, and climbed up into his van. Immediately she felt very uncomfortable. One thing she noticed was that there was a heavy smell inside the van. When they came to an intersection with a red light she grabbed the door handle on her side of the front seat and bolted away from the van. A few weeks later she saw an article in a local paper with a picture of the man who had offered her a ride. It was Ted Bundy, the serial killer of young women.

Medical personnel attacked:

Along Larimer Street late at night violence could take a number of different forms. One night the bartender at the tavern on 24th and Larimer asked me if I would go outside to observe what was happening. He was anxious about the welfare of a man who had been knifed in the tavern. The bartender had called 911. As I stepped outside I could see a man lying on the concrete sidewalk. Red blood was decorating the sidewalk near him. I watched as an emergency aid vehicle came to a top at the curb. Two medical technicians jumped out of the vehicle. There were men hanging around on the sidewalk in front of the tavern. These men attacked the med techs! I was walking these streets alone! Another night a man was shot in the back as he was leaving a tavern.

Men high on drugs:

On another night a man who seemed to be high on drugs approached me directly and when he saw my white collar he knelt down on the sidewalk to kiss my shoes! Later I saw the same man with two other men. This time they surrounded me, swearing that I was carrying something to protect myself. Two men searched me from in front, going through my pockets and patting down my coat. Another man walked around behind me, took my billfold out of a back pocket and then proceeded to remove all of my money (some $6 or $7 dollars) and then handed the billfold back to me. That night if I had hidden a knife or gun on my person I am sure that I would have been hit with it.

Lessons on self-protection:

Some nights I went into a neighborhood near East Colfax that had a reputation for violence. The parking lot of a 7/11 store in this area became a staging ground for a shootout one night. A tavern in this neighborhood became a frequent stop for me. The regular patrons occasionally directed solicitous comments on personal safety toward me. One stranger proceeded to lecture me on how to protect myself. He accentuated his remarks with demonstrations on such fine details as how to use a coat in self-defense against an attacker with a knife. Although he knew the language of self-defense he apparently was not able to follow his own advice. His jaw had been broken in a fight, teeth had been knocked out and ribs dislocated. He was looking for trouble and often found it. I went into the same places where he went but I was never attacked. In this tavern and in many places I visited at night, violence was a way of life. Those at highest risk were the people living in the area. Now the weapon of choice is guns, not knives.

A drive-by shooting:

Contact with some form of violence followed me wherever I did night ministry. In Tacoma, Washington a bartender asked me to visit her daughter who was in jail on a misdemeanor charge. I did make the visit during which this young woman shared her dreams about taking classes in a vocational school. She was released from jail a few days later. Late one night she was walking a few blocks away from where her mother worked when a car drove by, a window was opened, a gun came out and a shot was fired. The young woman was killed. I learned later that the killer actually had intended to shoot someone else. But the death of the woman and her dreams could not be recalled. I tried to console her mother.

More Encounters at Night

"I Have a Bottle of Pills"

Late one night in Denver a man called me wanting to talk. I met him in an all-night eatery where he had a cup of coffee and I drank hot tea. This man, Bill, was middle aged, average height and build. He was wearing a yellow shirt, decorated with some old brown stains. He immediately launched into his personal saga of defeat and desperation in his search for any kind of employment. He had been out of work for weeks and felt that he would never again be able to find a job. Then this man who was truly living in a bucket of depression shared with me his plan to take his life in suicide. At that time, it seemed like his only option. I encouraged him to continue looking for work. Then I made an appointment with him to see him a week later, same time, same place, adding that I wanted him to promise me that he would not take his life in the interim.

In our second meeting we talked more openly about suicide. I asked Bill how he planned to do this. He said that he had a bottle of pills. Then I gave him some more instructions. I told him that I wanted him to get those pills and throw them away, adding that I also wanted to watch him do it. We went out to the parking lot, got in our respective cars and I followed him to the apartment building where he lived with his wife. She was present when we climbed the stairs to their place. Their small apartment was shrouded in depression. I watched as Bill went into a bedroom, coming out with a bottle of pills. I then watched as he threw the pills into the sink and turned on the garbage disposal (not a recommended way to dispose of medicines today).

A week later I received another call from Bill. He invited me to their place for lunch. When I arrived the change in atmosphere was palatable. They were both expressing some hope, some joy. Bill had found a job. He was wearing a clean Texaco shirt. But he had not yet had a pay-check. His wife had prepared some canned soup and cheap sandwiches for lunch. When I looked at her left hand I could see that she was not wearing her wedding ring. Then I learned that she had hocked the ring to buy the meager food for the lunch. Her way to say Thank You!

"Can I help you?"

This was the mantra for Steve. I met him in the tavern I mentioned on East Colfax where another man tried to coach me on personal safety. An alcoholic, Steve lived in a cheap apartment conveniently located just above the tavern. One night he invited me to climb the stairs with him up to his apartment, indicating that he wanted to talk "more freely" than possible in the tavern. As I sat in an old hard-backed wooden chair, Steve immediately went to a small refrigerator in the room and returned with a soft drink for me. After we talked for a few minutes and after I had sipped the soft drink, Steve insisted on taking me down a dark, dirty hall to meet one of his friends. This friend, an elderly man, was a prisoner in his small rented room. He was a late-stage alcoholic. When I saw him he was wearing a ragged undershirt as he sat beside a wooden table drinking wine from a paper cup. Steve informed me that this man seldom went out of his room. Helping him was one of the daily duties assumed by Steve.

Steve had no strong church connections but he made it a point to emphasis how he always helped others. He was a major care giver for the apartment building. One of his major tasks was to ensure a regular flow of cheap wine from a near-by store to his fellow alcoholics. He was very busy, he told me, on the day when the Social Security and SSI checks arrived in the mail. For me the most impressive meeting with Steve was the time I saw him in the county jail. He was being held on a charge of stealing a pack of cigarettes from one of the largest chain grocery stores in the city. I did not tell him that the chain store he mentioned had been co-founded by one of my relatives. By the time I discovered that he was in jail and made my visit he had been in jail for 30 days. He could not raise the $10 for bail. He was very surprised to see me. I called the Public Defender's office after my visit and Steve was released the next day.

Black tights and leather belt:

One night in the same tavern where I met Steve, I talked with a middle-aged woman after she noticed my I.D. badge as I sat at the bar drinking a Coke. Sarah said that she knew about Operation Nightwatch from the time she had lived in Seattle. She had many conversations with the Director of Seattle's program. When we met she seemed truly overwhelmed by the steady beating of problems she encountered after moving from Seattle to Denver. Sarah continued the conversation as we walked together away from the bar to sit in a booth near the tavern's juke box. The sounds and vibrations from a popular country western song provided background music for our conversation.

The first issue Sarah wanted to talk about was the familiar refrain of financial problems that had haunted her since her arrival in Denver. As I have seen many times, people seem to be very open about their behavior and their fears when speaking privately to someone "of the cloth." In Sarah's case she freely admitted that when she could not get any form of financial assistance she started stealing from local food stores. One of her regular practices was to hide steaks under her coat and then casually stroll out of the store. This attracted the attention of store employees who notified the police. She was escorted by a uniformed officer to a waiting police car and given a free ride to jail. Although I really did not need the details, she did describe for me in considerable detail her body search at jail which she considered to be an "invasion of privacy." Her life of crime continued after she was released from jail. When she found a job at a junk yard and discovered that the owner could not read she proceeded to steal from him by telling him check amounts that were not accurate.

The black tights and leather belt came into the conversation as Sarah explained how she sold her body to get money. I think that she was building a good case for the fact that she was beyond the reach of God's love, something I had heard from many others. When she was particularly desperate for money a man offered her $75. First he asked her to put on a pair of black tights. When she was seductively dressed in this outfit with her bare breasts on full display the man removed all of his own clothes. Then he handed her his heavy, leather belt and told her to hit him with it. She compiled and eared her $75. But she was not proud of her role in this twisted scene.

As we talked in the tavern, Sarah spoke very sincerely about her desire for forgiveness. She said that she carried a bottle of water from Seattle, calling it her "holy water." But she got little consolation from this bottle. We talked of God's redemptive love, a topic she was not unfamiliar with given her contacts out in Seattle with Operation Nightwatch. With a country western tune playing on the juke box, I invited Sarah to look to God in prayer. I prayed and then instructed her to lift her concerns and guilt to God in prayer. At least for a brief moment that tavern in one of the roughest parts of downtown Denver became a sacred place.

"You gotta meet my wife:"

One night along East Colfax I met Jack, a 55-year-old man standing outside a tavern. As I passed him I said "how're you doing." Jack was eager to talk about his situation. In language that staggered with the insult of a recent indulgence in cheap wine, Jack informed me that he had been 86'd from the tavern. They would not let him in because he had a reputation for creating a disturbance. He informed me that he was a "good man." After we chatted for a few minutes on the sidewalk Jack said that he wanted me to follow him home so that I could meet his wife.

Together we crossed East Colfax in the middle of the block. I followed Jack as he made his way down an alley toward a large apartment building. On the back porch of this building he stopped in front of a small door to something resembling a broom closet. He opened this door. As I stood looking over his shoulder I could see the tattered clothes, long beard and glassy-eyes of a middle-aged man collapsed into a fetal position in the narrow confines of the box-like closet. Jack mumbled a greeting, took a new bottle of wine out of a coat pocket and handed it over to the gaunt figure in the box on the porch of the apartment building. The recipient of this largess carefully closed his fingers around the bottle. He never uttered a word. Jack closed the small door with a comment about "keeping a friend alive."

Once inside the apartment building I followed Jack up a flight of stairs and down a carpeted hall. He stopped in front of one door and knocked. A woman's voice came through the door. Jack said that he had a friend. The woman inside said that she did not want to meet any of his friends. He persisted and she finally opened the door. When she saw my clergy collar she immediately apologized to me, saying that Jack often brought his drinking buddies home. The apartment was pleasantly furnished and comfortably warm. The woman, his wife, was smartly dressed and a sharp contrast to the disheveled appearance of Jack.

After introductions, Jack began a long tirade against the woman who sat beside him in her cotton housecoat. He said that his wife would not help him. He blamed her for all of his problems. He just did not know what to do about her. At some point in the talking she asked me to "pray for them." I first spoke directly to her and then prayed.

When Jack ran out of energy for verbal abuse his wife spoke in a level, controlled voice. She said that I should hear her side of the story. That very week she had returned home from a period of hospitalization. The trip to the hospital in an emergency vehicle followed a severe beating from her husband during one of his drunken binges. Some 17 stitches were needed to close an open cut. In sharp contrast to his accusations against her, she informed me that she was the one who worked cleaning houses to pay the rent and keep them in food. He was not able to hold a job with his full-time commitment to alcohol. She said that she herself was a recovering alcoholic. She was fearful of how much longer she could keep going to AA with the kind of abuse she suffered at his hands. His regular physical beating of her seemed to be his major contribution to the marriage. Jack did not have a ready response to this reality confrontation.

After leaving the apartment that night I was determined to make another visit without the husband. A few days later in the afternoon I did return. The woman was home alone. She was glad to see me. Her first comment was that she felt that I had "really blessed" their home when I prayed during the late-night visit. We talked about her options. She felt that she could get a better job, but was hesitant about how to handle her alcoholic husband. I gave her strong support to leave him if necessary to protect herself. She had considered separation but needed reinforcement for taking such a move in the expression of "tough love." I told her that she was important and that I did not want to see her destroyed by the increasingly severe beatings her husband gave her on a regular basis. This story ends here. Like so many other encounters of the night I was left and remain left with s sense of mystery about what happened to this man and woman. This is not the way for a story to end.

Back in Vietnam:

One night I was walking along East Colfax on a Fourth of July Week end. Some fire crackers were going off near the downtown Denver streets. As I walked along I saw a man who was not wearing a shirt standing off by himself. When a load noise maker went off in celebration of the holiday this man ran in a panic to the brick wall of a building and started to pound the bricks with his fists. As I approached him he stated to talk about Vietnam. With the extra noise around him he was tossed back in his mind to the times of killing in Vietnam. He talked about the children and women who were killed. The term was not yet popular but he was experiencing post-traumatic stress disorder (PTSD). I told him to go and get a shirt to wear and that I would take him to the VA hospital. He did get the shirt and I did transport him to a place where they could help him through the crisis.

A loaded gun:

When I was sitting at the bar in a tavern on Larimer Street late one night someone came up behind me and said in a low voice that he wanted to talk. I turned to see a Native American, his long black hair tied up in a knot at the back of his head with a rubber band. I walked with him over to a booth in a dark corner of the tavern.

His first question for me was, "should I marry my girlfriend?" We talked briefly about this. Then Jonathan started talking about the major reason for his eagerness to talk with me. He said that he had been thinking of "ending it all." To be more specific, he said that he had often taken his gun, placed it on the kitchen table and then thought about shooting his girlfriend and then himself.

Jonathan then told me that he was on "downers." He was also having a beer, a potentially dangerous combination. While we talked he reached up to untie the rubber band holding his hair in place. The long, black hair fell below his shoulders. His speech was slow and studied, matching his total actions. While he continued talking Jonathan said that he had a 38 pistol tucked into his boot right there in the booth. Then he added that he had three cartridges in the gun, one was for his girlfriend, one for himself and one for a third party he did not identify.

Knowledge that this man held a loaded gun changed the options for me. When he said that he had been a VA patient I made a call to the local VA hospital, trying to set up an appointment for him. While I was on the telephone in the tavern some of his friends came by and he left with them. There was not a great deal I could do since he had a gun. I was thinking of my own safety. I could not offer to give him a ride to an ER room or some other facility. All professionals, including ministers, are mandated to report situations of grave danger. In this case I had to immediately assess the degree of danger to the person, to myself and to the program as well as the long-term effectiveness of the emergency response system. It was my decision at the time to move on to another place when the man drifted away from me. In retrospect perhaps it was the best decision because there was no murder-suicide.

Dean C. Jones

"Will you pray for our son, Running Bear?"

The long reach of decades of cultural struggle between Native Americans and those who came to this country from Europe caught up with me one night in a tavern along Larimer Street. I was pulled into a booth to sit in front of a man who was sitting beside a woman. He told me that he was a Native American and proud of it. Then he went into a tirade about how the "White Man" had disgraced his people with their religion, adding that now he had one of "them" right here in front of him. As he went on, criticizing me and the religion I represented the woman sitting beside him asked simply if she could say something. Then she asked a favor of me, saying "Can you pray for our son, Running Bear." So there in that booth in that tavern I prayed for Running Bear.

To Church

There will always be a need for special, even sacred spaces and places. There will also always be a need for some way for people to connect with who they really are. We have seen a major change in wearing apparel over the years. Casual has become the "in" choice. It is not unusual for men and women to be seen in church wearing blue jeans. But touching the kind of reality shared in this book remains removed from the formality of most times of corporate worship. One response could be that problems like chemical dependency are simply not inclined to be sitting in church pews. But I know that serious problems cannot be shut out by simply closing the church doors at the start of a formal worship service. The daily challenges for someone who is a recovery alcoholic and the bucket of pain carried by someone who has lost a family member by suicide do not melt away by walking through church doors.

Should the sacred place of worship give any time for comments about non-sacred but very serious personal and social problems? It would be impossible to live anywhere in our country today and not know that our world now faces many challenges. From major war in the Middle East to other forms of crisis such as the spread of EBOLA in West Africa. Within the protected boundaries of our country many experience major pain and loss. A recent study by the Centers for Disease Control and Prevention, for example, reported that in 28 key states the number of heroin related deaths doubled between 2010 and 2012, going from 1,779 to 3,665. It is difficult to measure the number of children and families in our country who do not have adequate food and/or housing. Programs such as the Operation Nightwatch work now serving people in Seattle and Portland are very important.

A Last Look at Denver

I was never able to launch a sustainable effort in Denver. I did try, pulling together a Board of Directors and recruiting a few clergy volunteers. But finances were always a problem. After only one year I left to continue my work at night in St. Louis, Missouri. This came when Stella accepted a position to teach at Greenville College in Greenville, North Carolina. Greenville is 53 miles from St. Louis. This became a regular commute for me.

Although I was "working" to start a new program of night ministry in Denver I was actually out of work since I was not receiving a salary. Our country is now climbing out of the recent recession. The unemployment rate is around 5%. People are finding jobs. But for some there are still fairly fresh memories of standing in an unemployment line. Of course job opportunities today vary with age and type of experience. For those who are under 24 or in their 50's, 60's or 70's the prospects are gloom. Many face the cold reality that there may not be real employment for them. In Denver some thirty years ago a long line of the unemployed formed outside of the Downtown Job Service Center in warm weather and then wound through basement hallways during the cold, winter months. I was part of this line for a few months. I reported every week for a few weeks and then once a month after the initial reporting period. If I went early enough to be one of the first in line the ordained visit took only an hour or two. During this time, I had ample opportunity to reflect on the whole scene.

It does not feel good to make a public display of the reality that you are not worth much in the machinery of the working world. I was not unusual in comparing myself to others. I had a lot of time to do this as I stood in line. I was on display but so were the people on this scene who held paying jobs. I was constantly reminded that people with what appeared to be average ability or even less were working for the State as security guards or interviewers while I was unable to find work. It is not particularly inspiring to start the day's search for work surrounded by people who are drawing unemployment because they cannot find work.

As I have shared, before this time in Denver to start a night ministry I had built up a fairly good resume in the area of work. I started working part-time when I was in high school. I managed to find and to keep fairly good full-time jobs while completing undergraduate and graduate degrees in college. For a few years I was looked up to with respect in small towns as the local pastor. Before my shadow life drawing unemployment I had held academic positions in universities for 13 years. I had a PhD in sociology from one of the leading universities in the nation. This became trivia flying in the wind when it came to working in the present. My background did not help in the desert of unemployment. I became very discouraged as I learned directly, not from books, that people with specific job skills were more likely to find work than I was.

During my time of unemployment, I became very disillusioned about the whole process. One of the disturbing realities was that there was very little connection between the formal demands of the Job Service Center and the actual process of getting a job. Special employment "counselors" at the Center were no help whatsoever. They simply flipped through a microfiche listing of job openings and then signed one of many cards for continuing eligibility. The weekly reporting of places where I had looked for work was a crude formality. I wrote down places where I dropped by just for the purpose of putting something on the form. My actual job search was done apart from the bureaucratic system of the Job Service Center.

Another disturbing part of the whole experience was what it was doing within my family. Looking back, I deeply regret that there were no times for me to really express my feelings. At times there was a deliberate avoidance of the topic. My situation was very difficult for extended family members to relate to in any meaningful way. The family did not extend into the no-man's land of hard times. I lived in the box of unemployment alone and it was a lonely place.

I am sure that others going through such an experience can say with me that it is often the small things that become so very important. When someone openly expressed concern this was always appreciated. On the other hand, although I attended church every

Sunday during those difficult months I never heard a sermon that was particularly helpful to someone who was unemployed. One sermon, in fact, was a very negative experience for me. During his sermon, the minister went on about his fireplace, his large backyard and his pets. At the time I was worried about paying the rent on a small apartment. During this worship service and at other times I was hounded by the question, "Why me?" While going through this difficult time I gave two nights a week in volunteer service to the downtown Denver night community. I must admit that as one residual of my experience in those dark days I still recoil when I hear a minister use illustrations in a sermon that advertise a very affluent life style. I wonder how those sitting in the pews who are struggling with basic issues handle such references.

In thinking back about this period of my life I recall how devastating it was for me. My sense of self-worth was eroded. I was reminded daily of the reality that our society values people according to their respective place in the world of work. Other people my age were going to work. I had no job. I was out of place. I over-reacted to small insults to my ego. At the time I was staying near a private University that our two children had graduated from. One day I decided to spend a little time in the college library. But when I tried to get in I was told to produce some evidence of student or faculty status. When I was turned away from the welcome sight of stacks of library books I was both furious at the system and challenged again in terms of my personal worth. Although it has been years since those dark days I am still hounded by a degree of insecurity and by problems in looking too much at what others have in comparisons to me.

In the next chapter I share my experiences in St. Louis at night. One bright spot in my three years in St. Louis was that my wife held a teaching position at Greenville College in Greenville, Illinois. I again had a dream that I could start a program of Operation Nightwatch.

Chapter 5

Under the Gateway Arch In St. Louis, Missouri

The Gateway Arch, near the Mississippi River in St. Louis, has stood for years as a 630-foot-tall memorial to the exploration and settlement of the western part of our country. In the pioneer days many people traveled through St. Louis on their way to a new frontier. An important part of every arch is the essential, united continuity from one leg of the arch to the other. It would be impossible for an arch to stand with only one leg secured to the ground. This Arch became another kind of symbol on December 8, 2014 when the New Yorker magazine featured the work of artist Bob Staake on the cover showing a "broken arch." Here the Arch stands open in the middle with one leg white and the other black. This was offered as a symbol of a country divided after a Grand Jury failed to find any reason to charge White police officer Darren Wilson with any crime after he shot and killed an 18 year old Black youth, Michael Brown in Ferguson Missouri, not far from the Arch. National marches in protest followed and were intensified when a New York Grand Jury likewise found another White police officer, Daniel Panteleo not guilty in the chokehold death of 43 year old Eric Gardner, a Black father of six children. The drumbeat of a nation divided continued on into the spring of 2015 in different cities following the death of Freddie Gray, a 25-year-old Black man while in police custody on April 19 in Baltimore, Maryland.

If we can take a leap back to the time before high-profile killings and a creative artist's depiction of the Arch, we can use it as a point of reference for other important realities. As I shared above, the Gateway Arch in St. Louis has stood as an important reminder of the time of new exploration and settlement in our country. It is very hard for me to imagine a time when the first settlers on the east coast had never seen the scenic beauty or experienced the new opportunities waiting in the western part of what we now take for granted as the United States. I am sure that those who saw the Colorado Rockies, Mt. Rainier or the seductive call of the Pacific Ocean for the first time were truly amazed.

Today the Arch remains as a clarion call to new frontiers, to changes, in our own life and in the life of others and in our country. Change, reaching for new goals is built into some of the systems of our society. Educational organizations, for example, exist to move students along a road to something new and different. No college or university could long exist if it had as a major goal to keep students where they were when they entered. How much can people change? How much do we expect them to change? These are important questions for any program reaching out to people at night or during the day.

Some changes are trivial, such as the change from preferring vanilla ice cream to chocolate ice cream. Other changes are monumental. When a person is in deep depression and thinking of suicide, for example, a move out of this state is essential. Can we change? It is much more difficult when resources are limited as in the case of someone who is alone and homeless downtown at night. Touching individuals is very important, always with some thought about how an immediate situation might be different. I am thankful that I was able to reach out to others at night on an individual level. But the sociologist in me knows that much more than individual change is needed. There will always be a need to look closely at those social systems which only perpetuate the problems seen at night.

One frontier that must be given more attention is the dynamic of change for seniors. Is it possible for anyone who is in the category of a "senior" to change his/her goals, ideas or relationships? With the growing numbers of seniors in our country this is an important question. At my age of 83 I can relate to this arena of change. I see some colleagues who are stuck in old ways, afraid of the new. This applies to much more than the apprehension over new computer technology.

Another important part of considering a new frontier is the role of waiting, of becoming prepared, of moving at the right time. Sometimes the meetings with strangers at night can serve as a time to help people recognize that a major change of some sort might not be beneficial. Problems can develop, for example, when people do not give adequate time and attention to the need for bereavement after the death of a significant other. The first step in this case might be participation in a bereavement class or group. Another way to discuss "change" is to realize that considerable energy can emerge from the experience of simply embracing the "now" and not eagerly marching on to new vistas. As I write this I am thinking of a new group I am part of at the West Boulder Senior Center in Boulder, Colorado. Here we hold up the value of contemplative living. Not unlike many other similar groups we look to Centering Prayer, Meditation and the works of Thomas Merton. Sitting, not walking or running, but simply being in the moment and perhaps allowing the refreshing sights and sounds of nature to embrace us can be a form of true inspiration. This also invites an openness to forms of spirituality that spring from a wide variety of religions expression far beyond the familiar retrains of Christianity.

Running Near St. Louis

When we moved to Greenville, Illinois I carried with me both a desire to continue my work in night ministry and a pair of well-worn running shoes. We rented a house from the college, giving us both a place to sleep and eat as well as a place for me to shower after my daily runs. My running took me, with some expenditure of energy, out of town as I ran on country roads near farm fields. In 1984 some farmers in the area were struggling to survive. Many lived on land handed down to them from former farmers in their family. The title to some farms made the tearful trip back to a local bank. Some farmers did not plant corn. Instead they carved their names on an unpopular roster of men and women who took their life in suicide.

During my tenure in Greenville and St. Louis I did complete two long distance events. I have no plaques, no memorabilia from these events. Both were done to promote my new program in St. Louis. My first challenge was to cover the 53 miles from Greenville into St. Louis. I was very familiar with this route since I drove the distance regularly as I went into St. Louis in my work of night ministry. I started out early on a Saturday on the day of my run. I carried a bottle of water and some Gatorade in a holder around my waist. Stella drove our car, following me over the distance. After leaving the city streets around the college my course took me out to highway 127, then I ran on the shoulder of highway 70 and finally 70 and 40. Most of the 53-mile distance was near open fields. I never ran through any towns. I was impressed by the sight of some mounds of earth near Collinsville, Illinois. This was the site of the Chokia Mounds State Historic Park. This part of our country was very different back in the day when these mounds were an important part of Native American culture.

The mounds were built between A.D. 1050 and A.D. 1350. They were for Native American rituals and elite tombs. It is very hard to imagine what the present route into what is now the city of St. Louis was like back then. We take for granted major highways and fast cars. I continued on west of the mounds, crossing the Mississippi River on the Eads Bridge to end up under the Gateway Arch in downtown St. Louis. A few people from Greenville College were on hand to congratulate me. On another occasion I completed a 50 mile course just west of downtown St. Louis. This was also to promote my work at night. It was the first such event for me in which someone else also ran the entire distance. This other runner was a young student attending the college in Greenville. He ran track and field in school and came in shortly before me as a few people waited for us at the finish area.

Walking the Streets of St. Louis at Night

Bag lady:

Martha was a bag lady. I first met her late one night when she was sitting inside the Greyhound Bus Depot in downtown St. Louis. With thinning strands of grey hair and weathered face she fit the stereotype of "frail and elderly". I would learn later that she was 92 years old. Titles tell us something about someone's associations. The titles "Teacher," "Student," "Mother" or "Grandmother" for example, immediately connote relationships. In St. Louis at night the title "Bag Lady" was a term of derision. In the rush of life in the city, a bag lady was regarded as worth little. Like a shopping bag, she was something to be discarded, tossed away with no intrinsic value. This was someone who was homeless, someone with no meaningful significant others in her life. She always carried bags, stuffed with her personal effects.

At our first meeting Martha was sitting alone in a booth in the restaurant part of the downtown Greyhound Bus Depot. Her faced was lined with the cares of life. I could easily imagine how she earned her physical marks of aging. She was a mother and a grandmother. She had known long hours of working to make life comfortable for her son and daughter. Now she was downtown late at night alone. When Martha told me where she had lived I made a special trip out to her former place of residence during the day, hoping to find some of her family. I did locate the address and talked with some in the neighborhood. But I never located family. A new fast-food place dominated the place which once held her house. I think that it is possible that her family had, unfortunately, engaged in elder abuse involving finances.

At our first meeting in the Greyhound Bus Depot, Martha was eating chocolate covered raisins. She offered me some when I sat in the booth across from her. We ate together and talked. I was told that her husband had died. Before his death he told her that he wanted to take her on a trip. Perhaps the hours she was spending in downtown bus depots was her way to maintain contact with the dream of a trip with him. She said that she watched carefully for times when the women's restroom was free from the supervision of someone working for the depot and then hurried in to do her personal washing in this room.

As I saw Martha on the street at night I watched as things went from bad to worse for her. I was never successful in contacting her children. At times she would talk to me and at other times she turned away from me, refusing all attempts on my part to communicate. One night she asked me if I was married. When I said "yes" she wanted to know why I was not home with my wife. She said that I was a poor husband and turned her back to me. A few nights later she seemed especially distressed, informing me that someone had taken her purse and all of her money. I gave her a few dollars to carry her through the night until she could contact another resource in the morning.

One very hard episode for me was the time when Martha was taken to the city's mental health facility. When I learned from my contacts on the street that she was in this place I went there to pay her a visit. She obviously recognized me but she would not talk to me. She sat in the main lobby of her ward, tearing Kleenex tissues into small pieces and stuffing these into her purse. She took a tube of bright, red lipstick and proceeded to smear the contents from one ear, down her face, under her mouth and then up to the other ear. After two weeks she was released but seemed far worse than before. She went from carrying two plastic bags to cradling four or five and was very withdrawn.

My last contact with Martha came on a cold St. Louis night during the winter. As I approached the Greyhound Bus Depot. around midnight I saw her coming out. It was customary for security guards to kick her out, regardless of the weather, because she never had a ticket. They did not want the depot to become a shelter for the homeless. There were no emergency shelters in the immediate downtown business core at that time.

As she stood with her tight fists held tight against her light coat in the cold of the night I told her that I would find her a place to sleep. Although she did not freely talk to me, she did take my hand when I invited her to do this. I held her hand as we walked together slowly across a downtown intersection. As we crossed with the light I noticed that she was having real difficulty determining the pattern of light changes in the darkness. I thought of the potential danger for her with this vision limitation as she walked from the Greyhound depot to the Trailways depot in the dark.

That night my car was not far away. I helped her into the front seat and stowed her bags in the back seat. After a short drive to one of the emergency shelters in St. Louis I helped her up a short flight of stairs. As we waited together for the door to open, Martha surprised me. It had been some time since she had voluntarily talked to me. Since her words were rare they were very valuable. Standing on the porch of that shelter she turned to me and gave me a word that will always remain with me. That word was simply "thanks." This has become a major memory for me. Maybe it speaks as well for a number of others I also helped late at night. It left me with a strong and positive reminder of a woman who was so much more than a "bag lady." After that event when I was out on a cold winter night I thought of Martha and hoped that she did get back in touch with her family. I never saw her again, leaving St. Louis shortly after that contact to continue my work at night in Tacoma, Washington.

An 8-year-old street person:

The streets at night do not discriminate. They will absorb anyone who comes their way. One night in St. Louis when I was out with one of my clergy volunteers we watched as a young boy, blue eyes and dirty face, played the video machines in a downtown bus depot. At first we thought that Tony was with some other boys. But when the older boys left he stayed, begging money so that he could play the machines again. When we were distracted by other situations and then looked for him again he had disappeared.

Since we knew where other video machines were located in the downtown area, we started again looking for Tony. It did not take long to find him. This time we took him aside and spent some time listening to his story. He had not been home from school. He was 8 years old. He was afraid that his father would beat him up again. He did not know what to do. He did warm up to the idea of a McDonald's kid meal. We purchased this food for him and then called the police and child protective services. We sat with Tony until the police came. In subsequent communication with the child protective service we learned that Tony and his family were well known to the agency. The father was an alcoholic. I am not sure how the situation was resolved by the agency. As I recall, there were 6 or 8 children in the family.

No money and no hope:

Another person of the night who will always haunt my memory is a homeless man I met one night in downtown St. Louis near the Gateway Arch. This was during a 4th of July celebration. The waterfront area was bright with happy crowds of revelers. Not far from this carnival atmosphere I saw a man sitting on a concrete stoop near the sidewalk. A large bag was propped up near him

I stopped to chat with this stranger. He had very little to say. I did learn that the plastic bag was full of soda cans. He had been collecting these cans all day. But city clean-up crews were on the scene before him so his efforts produced only one bag full of cans. I asked him how much he expected to get for these cans. He said "about $1.50." I gave him $1.00 to nearly double his earnings for the day. The most impressive part of this experience for me was the reaction on the part of this stranger to my gift. He gave no emotional response. He was so dejected that any addition to his meager resources just did not register. There was no word of thanks. His was a bare survival existence. There was no energy for emotional exchanges of any kind.

Drinking black coffee at 1 AM:

Today and back years ago when I was working in St. Louis underemployment is and was a more extensive problem than homelessness. When I think of underemployment I always think if Sam, a 61-year-old. I saw him many times in downtown St. Louis, often sitting in an all-night cafeteria staring at a cup of black coffee. His life was like drinking black coffee. There were no amenities, no sugar or cream, only the essentials. Usually Sam sat nodding in a semi-sleep state instead of actually drinking the coffee.

Some years before our meeting Sam was laid off after working for the same company for 25 years. The company had no retirement plan. Sam first exhausted all of his unemployment compensation and then started selling newspapers. As he explained to me, dishwashing at minimal wage for a few hours a week did not pay as much as selling papers.

Sam is an example of many folks who are working but not making enough to get by on. For him the work day began at 2AM when he was the first in line to pick up newspapers. His major selling time was between 6AM and 8AM when he covered some of the downtown office buildings. During the middle of the day he was able to get a little rest. Then he started selling again around 10PM. To boost his income, he sold his blood for plasma twice a week. All of his efforts did not net him enough to pay for a regular place to sleep. One of his personal goals was to make enough money each week so that he could stay in a cheap hotel over the weekend.

A rugged individualist, Sam refused to go to emergency shelters because, according to him, these places always have "body lice and lots of fights." He also tried not to go for free food because he felt that this might deprive someone who was needier. Sam was very bitter about people who get temporary help for such items as a fan or a heater for an apartment and then sell these items to buy "a beer or a joint."

The daily schedule for Sam was a little like the tiring routine of a shopping bag lady. He seldom got a regular period of unbroken sleep. When he had money he went to places where he could eat all he wanted for a set price. He drank a lot of coffee and dreamed of the time when he would be able to draw Social Security. On top of everything else, Sam was vulnerable to all of the dangers of the street.

Two years before our meeting Sam had a car and used it to sleep in at night. One night two men approached his car from either side with drawn guns. They took Sam's money but left him when he refused to crawl into the car's trunk. Sam had four other occasions when he was robbed during a period of four years on the street. One of these affairs included a frightful encounter with two youths who first took his money and then said that they were going to shoot him. Sam pleaded with them, asking why they wanted to kill him since they had all of his money. One of the two explained that he "just wanted to kill somebody." Fortunately, someone came along the street and the two youths ran away.

Helping a truck driver:

The variety of problems presenting at night is interesting. I found that late in the day people seldom asked for money. They were more inclined to be thinking of something else that was important to them. In St. Louis I regularly transported homeless strangers to local shelters. In the process I became involved with a variety of problems that these folks staying at the shelter were concerned about. On one occasion one of the men at a shelter was an experienced truck driver. He needed to go some distance from the downtown area for an interview so that he could get back to work. I offered to give him a ride. He was very middle-aged and walked with a noticeable limp from an old injury to his left leg. At the truck facility I waited while he took a formal, written exam. I was a little anxious for him when

I noticed that younger, able-bodied men were also applying for the job. I assumed that they could do better on a paper and pencil test. After the written exam my friend pulled himself up into a tractor rig for a road test. He turned that powerful tractor around "on a dime," quickly demonstrating his driving skill. I was happy for him when he was told that he had the job. He was hired on the spot. I drove back downtown alone and never saw the man again.

"My wife is an alcoholic:"

One night I met Bill, a middle-aged man, wearing blue jeans and a clean T shirt, in the Greyhound Bus Dept. downtown. He was alone and he wanted to talk He was walking through the depot and said that he was headed for some place out of town. His major concern was his wife's excessive drinking. She often became abusive toward him when she was drunk. One of his coping strategies was to get away from her by taking long walks. I listened and tried to be supportive of him in his situation. One of my specific suggestions for him was that he should get involved in Alanon. I was surprised when he said that he had never heard of this organization. Alanon has a long history of helping the family and friends of alcoholics.

Talk of suicide in an affluent cocktail lounge:

Problems can be found in any part of town. Someone who will listen is always needed. In St. Louis one night I was out of the downtown business core where I usually made my rounds. For some reason I was out by the airport and decided to stop at an up-scale cocktail lounge. I sat at the bar and ordered a soft drink. Before I could finish this drink a man sitting a few bar stools from me moved closer and ordered another Coke for me. He wanted to talk.

This stranger was not homeless. He was a commercial pilot with one of the major airlines. He was in St. Louis for only one day to attend the funeral of a buddy who had taken his own life in suicide. The pilot needed to talk about his experience. At one point in our conversation he asked me if I knew what it was like to sit through a closed casket service with a room full of strangers. One of his major concerns was how to talk about this with his young daughter. He so much wanted her to find happiness, hope and a true reason for living. This was the major topic for our sharing. I was thankful that I had both some academic and practical experience around suicide.

"My pastor is an alcoholic:"

Sometimes in St. Louis I began the night shift at the Sheraton Hotel in the cocktail lounge. I talked with the bartender as I waited for a clergy volunteer who was on duty for that night. This spotless bar, managed by a formally attired bartender, was hard for me to get used to after the round of skid row bars I had seen in other cities. On my first visit to this cocktail lounge I stared in amazement at the sight of a fancy dishwasher in motion. As the glasses from the bar were washed to a spotless sparkle I could not help thinking of a bar in Portland, Oregon where cockroaches danced in the semi-darkness. In that bar the bartender once informed me that a customer had been stabbed in the back while sitting where I was sitting and that this man was now a quadriplegic. The Sheraton Lounge was indeed a very different kind of place for me.

But no place at night or during the day is above the possibility for major personal problems. In the fancy lounge one night I met John, a business man who was wearing a dark, three-piece suit. He was staying at the Sheraton while looking for work. When I appeared to be someone who would listen, he talked on and on about his personal situation. For starters, he informed me that he was separated from his wife and that a divorce was pending.

As John saw his situation, his work stress and other sources of stress had been too much for the marriage. One of his major areas of stress, as he saw it, was his own involvement in the lives of other people. He said that, as one example of this, he had spent too much time trying to help his pastor who was an alcoholic. This pastor did get professional help, with John's assistance. But his own marriage was shattered. Now he was trying to pull his own life back together again.

On that particular night some volunteers would be meeting me at the Sheraton before going out on the street. This group included a Catholic priest, a Presbyterian pastor and a Lutheran pastor. I invited John to join the group for prayer in a corner of the cocktail lounge. He was glad for this opportunity. After the prayers one of the volunteers stayed with him for three hours to help him sort out his situation.

Coffee and deep depression:

I ordered one of my favorite drinks, hot chocolate, in an all-night restaurant in St. Louis one night and then sat near others who were having coffee. Since I had been in this place before, the waitress knew me and the kind of work I did. She told me that a young woman sitting across the room by herself seemed very disturbed. I took my cup of hot chocolate over to where she was sitting at a small table and sat opposite her. She immediately started talking to me about her situation. She said that she had been living on her own recently and felt that this had been going fairly well. But over the last couple of days she started going into a state of deep depression. She was thinking of suicide.

When this woman told me that she had been a patient at the State Hospital I told her that it sounded to me like she needed to go back to the hospital. She agreed that this would be good. I called the hospital. They pulled her record and told me to bring her over. I completed this chance encounter by driving the woman to the hospital and watching as they re-admitted her.

Manic depression:

The term "bi-polar" is more popular today. But the symptoms and associated problems are the same. One night in St. Louis when I was walking through the Trailways Bus Depot I noticed a well-dressed man in his 50's pacing the floor from one end of the depot to the other. I walked over to him and introduced myself. He said that his name was Jim, that he was from Ohio and that he was going out to California as part of some major enterprise. Then Jim said that he had been a professor of history with teaching experience at a major university. He then took out his wallet from a back pocket and showed me his identification cards from Blue Cross insurance and for membership in an association of people with manic depression. This became an introduction to his major problem at that time, he was going through a spell of acute agitation as part of his mental illness.

Given his high level of education and general intelligence, Jim was in touch with both his problem and appropriate professional help. He said that he wanted to talk with someone in a clinic which had connections with the Manic-Depressive Association. I did not know how to evaluate the availability of options at that hour of the night. I called one of the major local hospitals which had a special psychiatric unit. Jim hesitated about going there when I could not give him strong assurances about how they might respond to someone with a manic-depressive disorder. But after some discussion and with his rising state of agitation he agreed to take a chance. He felt that he could not just spend the night pacing the floor in a strange downtown bus depot.

The trip across town was one of those unusual experiences for me. I decided to pull out onto the freeway system which circled the city of St. Louis. After only a mile or two the far right lane came to an abrupt halt. Ahead red lights were flashing and a uniformed officer was directing traffic around the scene of an accident. I pulled over, stopped, got out of my car and ran ahead on foot to the scene to see if there was anything I could do. My help was not needed at the crash site. Jim sat in the front seat of my car, arms and legs moving in a rhythmic swaying of nervous tension. We hurried to the hospital, pulled up into the emergency entrance zone and walked inside. Unfortunately, this hospital did not have a psychiatric specialist on duty at the time. We left and drove to a second hospital some distance away.

Hospital shopping in the middle of the night is not an easy task. It is something that might be expected for someone who is family. But I had a stranger in the car. At the second hospital I did more than pull to a stop. I walked with Jim down long halls to a general reception area. After waiting for our turn we were informed that a resident in psychiatry was on duty and that he could see Jim. This resident did a very good job. He talked with Jim and then both of us together. Then he went into the details of medication and he also got the name of Jim's psychiatrist in Ohio. When he called this person he was given specific instructions on the best course of treatment for Jim. The most immediate need was for emergency shelter. On the following day plans would be made for Jim to return home. The hospital maintained a transportation system for all patients including those seen in the emergency room. When I was assured that they would follow-up on the need for a trip downtown to a shelter I left the hospital and returned to the downtown streets for more work.

I was so impressed by the excellent work of this hospital and the intern that I sent a letter to the person in charge of the psychiatric unit. In this letter I was very complimentary of the service given late at night. His reply was very disturbing to me. He was very condescending to me, a lowly minister. He questioned the process of me daring to imply that psychiatric services could be rated from poor to good or excellent. His strong message for me was that it was none of my business how well his professionals were doing since they always did excellent! When I read this letter I found myself wishing that he could confront the mental health system late at night in different cities as I had done. I was sure that things looked comfortable from his cozy office as he sat at his desk. But for people on the street at night good service was simply not to be taken for granted.

"I am Jesus:"

When I was working in St. Louis the City Hospital was across the street from the city's mental hospital, Malcolm Bliss. This created problems when patients who needed mental health care ended up at the wrong hospital. One night a young woman who seemed to be in a very severe state of confusion was waiting in the room adjacent to the emergency entrance at the City Hospital.

I was able to initiate interaction with this woman. Her name was Helen. She wore a multi-colored dress and carried a well-worn, black purse. One of her problems was that she could not get the receptionist to understand her. I volunteered to go up to the intake window with her to help her answer questions. The person doing intake for the hospital was very annoyed when Helen began to struggle over such simple questions as: "what is your most recent address?"

The hospital employee wanted everything to fit into neat spaces. She really had a problem when faced with something out of place. At one point she yanked the forms out of her typewriter with an oath and yelled that she had to account for "every carbon copy" she made. Mention of a typewriter really dates this memory. But back then these machines were an indispensable part of any office operation. I could see that the woman looking for help was really at the wrong hospital. She should have been across the street at the city's mental hospital. The police had dropped her off at the wrong place.

My next move was to walk Helen over to Malcolm Bliss. I waited with her in the waiting room as she smoked one cigarette after another. Then she fell asleep, leaning against me. When she woke up she looked directly at me and said that she was really Jesus. I was glad when her name was finally called. She left the waiting room for her interview with the resident on duty.

I assumed that my work would be over after the intake interview. I was sure that this very disturbed young woman would be taken in for the night at least. But that was not to be the case. When she appeared again in the waiting room I asked to see the resident who had interviewed her. He was primarily interested in her delusions. He never covered such basics as where she was living and never gave any consideration to where she might stay for the night. I was not happy with this turn of events. I strongly felt that her immediate need for shelter should have been given some priority.

Although Helen was not really the kind of person who would do well in a regular shelter because of her mental illness, I decided that I should try to find her a place for the night at least. I first drove her to a shelter not far from the hospital. A knock on the door and the ringing of a door bell finally aroused someone. But they had no room for another guest. After getting the same response from another emergency shelter, I took Helen back to the waiting room of the mental hospital, informing her that she might need to sit up in this room all night. It was now around 2:30AM. I could do no more because I had to get a little sleep before an early morning meeting.

"I am having a baby:"

When Jane made this statement she honestly felt that she was in the immediate process of giving birth. As she stood, talking to the person doing intake at the city's General Hospital, she could not understand why she was not immediately rushed into the delivery room. As I heard her and saw that she was, in reality, somewhat thin with absolutely no signs of carrying a baby, I knew that this was another case of someone who was at the wrong hospital.

My reaction was predictable. I took Jane by the hand and walked my well-worn path over to the city's mental health facility which was open all night. In that waiting room Jane was again very agitated. She honestly felt that she was giving birth. Again I waited as she went into the interview room with a psychiatric intern. I was again disappointed when she returned to sit beside me in the waiting room. The pattern with Helen was repeated. I am sure that the intern had good notes about her delusions. But again, there was no interest in her immediate situation in terms of housing.

The streets were now very familiar with my late-night forays trying to help people. I drove Jane to some possible shelters but again was unable to find a room. I had no other alternative but to take her back to the hospital. I guided her again to the intake area and told her that the hospital was open all night, suggesting that she simply sit in the waiting area until the light of another day. This was another night when I had serious misgivings about my ability to really help.

On The Road Again

After only two years in St. Louis I left the area to return to the Pacific Northwest. Someone donated special funds to Seattle's Operation Nightwatch to assist in the development of programs in other cities. Rev. Norm Riggins, the Director of Seattle's program, contacted me with an invitation to start a new work in Tacoma, Washington not far from Seattle. In St. Louis I was struggling to build a budget to cover my basic needs plus a small "salary." I could not refuse the offer of $11,000 to launch a new effort. The young Board of Directors for St. Louis attempted to select a new leader and to continue the work but they were no able to do this. The key factor in the St. Louis work was that my wife had taken the teaching position at Greenville College, covering our basic needs while I tried to generate a line of funding which was never adequate. Stella enjoyed her teaching role but also had strong feelings about the Seattle area. I suggested that perhaps I should make the move alone but she decided to go with me. As I share in the next chapter, it was in Tacoma that she surprised me with divorce papers.

During my writing of this chapter I had thought that I should enlarge the work to include, for example, some comments about the St. Patrick Center, a Catholic facility which graciously gave me office space. But my decision was, finally, that the chapter is best left alone as it is, a memorial to some very dear people it was my privilege to meet late at night near the Gateway Arch. Given the nature of my work I have never had the opportunity to know the long-range impact I may have made on the life of someone else. As you read this you may also think of some folks you have had contact with for only a fleeting time. I join you in wishing all the very best.

Chapter 6

Walking Where the Sails Met the Rails: Tacoma, Washington

A City on Puget Sound

In 1989 I worked with a number of others in the completion of a booklet with a number of historical photos titled: "Walking Where the Sails Met the Rails: A Venture into Tacoma's Past[3]." One of my motivations for this project was that it was planned as another way to raise funds for my work in Operation Nightwatch-Tacoma. Looking back 100 years ago, Tacoma was not just another city on Puget Sound. As Murray Morgan, noted historian of the area, notes in the introduction to the book, between the years of 1839 and 1889 the population of Tacoma increased from 1,000 to more than 300,000.

A combination of factors became important in the flowering of Tacoma. The Northern Pacific Railroad was completed in 1883. Ships were loading and unloading cargo going to and coming from distant ports around the world. Natural treasures including timber, lead, silver and gold passed through the rail and sail ports of the city.

My favorite story from the booklet is the tale of Jack, the beer drinking bear. This bear was captured as a cub and given to the old Tacoma Hotel as a mascot. He was taught to step up to the bar and drink beer from a mug. Fully grown and weighing some 800 pounds, Jack became a major attraction. Visitors and residents brought friends to the old hotel to watch the unusual sight of the beer drinking bear. But one-night Jack escaped from the hotel. A local policeman who was unaware of Jack's reputation and who was frightened at the sudden sight of a bear in the downtown area pulled his gun and fired. Jack was seriously injured and when it became obvious that he would not live, he was killed. His mounted replica stood in the hotel lobby for years to welcome visitors.

Over the years Tacoma did not become a serious challenger for the title of "jewel of the Puget Sound." Seattle became the dominate city. But Tacoma and Pierce County did sustain the kind of night life in the 1980's that called for serious work in night ministry.

Where Addiction, Heart Ache and Death Met the Clergy Collar: My Tacoma

As I have reinforced throughout this book, there is intrinsic value in each person. This is not based on what they have accomplished or their worth in the larger society. When I was invited to share a personal walk with someone it was like walking on sacred ground. I became different in the process. The encounters are much more than "stories." They are touched with the timeless heart-beat of eternity. Those I met at night will never be listed in some hall of fame. But they did have value. I lived with each of these very important people. I hope that you have been able to stay with the printed words on the pages of this book to imagine how the story played out in real life on a downtown street or somewhere else at night where few dare to tread.

Two for the road: Georgia and Jerry:

The first draft for this section of the chapter was: Cocaine and Heroin: Georgia and Jerry. It is all too easy to use labels. This couple was heavily addicted to drugs. But they were much more than addicts. They were real people with feelings and dreams and love for each other. I saw them often on the downtown Tacoma night scene. In her 40's, Georgia had lived in Washington all of her life, moving to Tacoma from the Tri-Cities area of the state. Jerry had lived most of his 40 years in Mexico; he was fluent in Spanish but struggled with English.

I first met Georgia when I was looking for someone to help me learn Spanish. A mutual friend introduced her to me as someone who was fluent in both English and Spanish. This turned out to be a very limited introduction to what she was familiar with. Her personal journey spanned much more than two languages.

Georgia was a frequent flyer in the skies of tragedy and trauma. As an indication of the turbulent nature of her life, she remembered the time of our first meeting as the time one of her friends shot and killed another friend. Her memory of that fateful night included going to the apartment of the man who had pulled the killing trigger. As she recalled, he was lying on top of the blankets on his bed with a pistol on his stomach, crying his eyes out. Georgia tried to comfort him. She remembered being in shock on the street when she turned and saw me, a stranger, wearing the clergy collar. I have no memory of that first sight of her. She said that she wanted to talk to me back then, but was afraid to.

The traumatic shooting event was in the past and not the most immediate pain for Georgia when we were formally introduced. Jerry had been picked up by the police and charged with possession of drugs. He was in jail. His involuntary isolation from society was especially painful for him because of his lack of fluency in English and separation from his significant other, Georgia. I offered to become a liaison, both with life outside the jail and with Georgia. Our first meeting was awkward, but when I mentioned Georgia and told him where she was he was notably lifted in spirits

It is hard to hide the insidious marks of drug use on body and spirit. During my first visit with Jerry I noticed that his body was tattooed with skin sores form the use of needles. He was in jail for 40 days and I saw him regularly during this time. Sometimes he came for our visit with medication covering his sores. They did heal. In jail his general physical condition seemed to improve.

His major problem behind bars was that he did not always know where Georgia was. He could show deep depression and this was most often on display when I told him that it was hard for me to keep in touch with her. Sometimes I saw her on the street. I knew that she was staying in a cheap hotel downtown. I delivered messages between the two when this was possible. Georgia did not try to get on his list of visitors. She was herself too often a resident behind the uncompromising iron bars herself

While Jerry was in jail he was escorted into court for a hearing. I attended this hearing with Georgia. An interpreter was available. This was an unequal contest. The defense attorney assigned by the court was bi-lingual. But the judge did not understand Spanish. It was interesting to observe his actions and to hear him talk about Jerry. During his verbal dialogue about the case he defined Jerry as "someone with a third grade education." After the hearing Georgia said that she was very angry over the assessment of the judge. She said that she felt that the judge was making a hasty evaluation based upon his own inability to understand Spanish. Jerry was, in fact, fairly well educated. He could read very well. But he could not speak or read English very well.

The judge also expressed the conviction that Jerry would never be able to pay any fine so the only way to get anything out of him was to keep him in jail. Jerry's sentence was set, based on the "fact" that he had a prior offense on the books. It turned out that this information was false since Jerry was working at the time of the alleged former offense. His name happened to be a very common name in Mexico.

I learned more about Georgia as I kept in touch with her. She confided in me that she was on cocaine. She also talked about her deep feelings for Jerry and her anxiety about his welfare. She seemed to be willing to do almost anything to raise money to get him out of jail. When I pressured her about getting into treatment she said that she had some legal things to take care of and that she needed to raise money for Jerry.

There were times when Georgia appeared haggard and thread bare. Other times there seemed to be a little hope. One night she asked me to take her to McDonald's for some food. She had money. She ordered and paid for a large amount of Chicken McNuggets for herself and a cup of hot chocolate for me. I had learned that such a display of money meant only one thing, she was again into drug dealing. A few weeks after the McDonald's visit Georgia told me that she had reached the point where her demand for cocaine had reached a crisis point. Her habit cried out for several hundred dollars every day. She told me that she deliberately selected drug dealing as the way to raise this money. As she explained to me, there were other things she could do to get money but she felt that selling drugs was "the least damaging to others."

Two days before Jerry was released from jail, Georgia was picked up by the police. It took me four days to find her in jail because she had used a different name when she was picked up. This time, on my first visit, Georgia was in the middle of withdrawal. She was very sick. As she sat across from me in the interview room, I noticed that her arms were covered with bruises and scars. She was barefooted. She shook all over. During my next visit she was over most of the chilling but had moved into a period of deep depression. She expressed doubt that she would ever see Jerry again. She felt strongly that she would be taken to prison again. Then she said that she had been in prison before for three years, and at that time was really "burned out."

Georgia really felt that this was the end for her. In addition to her own problems, she said that her mother was dying or near death and she could not see her. During this visit I took off my coat and placed it around her shoulders when I saw that she was cold and shaking. I talked openly with her about suicide. When I left she affirmed that suicide was not the option for her.

Two days after this jail visit Georgia was transported to a city some 200 miles away, but still in Washington. This other city had a warrant out for her over an unpaid fine of some $350. Given her condition the last time I saw her, I felt obligated to visit her in the new jail. I found Jerry on the street and invited him to make the four-hour trip with me to see her. We arrived only minutes before the visiting time was over. She was very happy to see Jerry. We were told that she would be going to court that very night. She was hopeful that she would be released on the spot because Jerry had $175 and she had $40 for a total of about half of the money needed. I waited around in the small town with Jerry for the late-night court session.

As it turned out, Georgia was brought into court as the only woman with eight other inmates. They were led into the court in lock-step, hand-cuffed with a strong rope strung between each pair of hands. Georgia would later confide to me that this was a very dehumanizing experience. Georgia did poorly in court. She was very bitter and challenged the judge about her fine and days in jail. The judge took a very negative approach to the case, insisting that she remain in jail to do the 15 days as sentenced. Georgia was crushed at these words. We watched as she was led back to jail. After this scene we drove through the night, getting back to Tacoma at 3:30 AM the next day.

After that long night I lost track of Jerry on the downtown streets. Five days later I received a call from Georgia in Seattle. She had been able to talk friends and family members into paying the total fine and giving her bus fare out of town as far as Seattle. I drove up and gave her a ride the rest of the way back to Tacoma. It seemed impossible to find Jerry. Georgia was now determined to get off cocaine. We asked around on the street and a friend of hers told us that Jerry was staying in one of the old hotels in town. I went with her to the place. She stayed in the hotel lobby while I went up to his room. In my limited Spanish I told him that "a friend" was down in the lobby and that this friend wanted to see him. This was the way she wanted me to announce her presence. He dressed quickly and followed me down the steps of the hotel. I watched as they embraced and walked out of the hotel lobby arm, in arm, together again after two months of separation.

A week passed before I heard from Georgia again. When I finally heard from her, she invited me out to dinner. She and Jerry were staying in a cheap motel near the downtown drug strip. I drove them to a Chinese restaurant and they paid for an expensive, family-style dinner. Back in the motel room I became aware that Georgia did not have basic items of clothing when two friends of hers came by to give her and Jerry some clothes. The irrational spending of money is one of the characteristics of addiction.

When Georgia stepped outside to talk with her friends, Jerry went into the bathroom. When he came out his behavior changed. He locked the door and pulled a chair up under the doorknob. Then he pulled the window shades closed and yanked a metal covering off a heat vent so that he could stare at the exposed wires. From his words I gathered that he was seeing bugs or something else hiding in the piece of metal. When Georgia returned to the room her first question was whether or not he had been to the bathroom. When I told her that he had she immediately cussed him out for "shooting up" while a "priest" was around. During this heated exchange I noticed the point of a needle sticking out of his back pocket.

Georgia was thrown into a fit of despair, crying as she said that she just could not stay with him through the night when he was acting like this. She said that he had enough heroin in the room and that he would just keep shooting up until it killed him. During these tense minutes, Jerry expressed a desire to talk with me. Georgia interpreted for him as he spoke in Spanish. He said that he wanted help in getting off drugs and then added that Georgia was also "sick."

I called a detox facility located some 180 miles away in Eastern Washington. No such facility was available at that time in Tacoma. I asked the facility east of the mountains to hold two beds and then offered this as an option to the couple. Georgia again served as my interpreter in discussing this with Jerry. After some delay they agreed to go with me. Her words at the time implied that she was at the end of her rope.

It was now 1:30 AM. I had been going all day. But they loaded up their few personal effects and we started off on a four-hour drive through the darkness over a mountain pass to Wenatchee, Washington. There was time for a lot of talk during the trip. At one point Georgia said that she was very thankful for what I had done for both of them but that she just did not understand why I was doing it.

We stopped at a 24-hour restaurant in a small town on the way for some coffee. Georgia went into the women's restroom. When she finally returned to the car she said that she had done something that was "very hard to do." Then she asked me if I had any idea what it was like to flush $800 worth of drugs down the toilet.

At 6: AM we parked in front of the drug treatment place. This was an emotional parting. I was very tired after driving all night. Georgia said that she would not be able to make it without God's help. I prayed with her, tears in my eyes. They gathered up three plastic bags of personal effects and I walked with them into the facility where I left them after a final round of hugs. I drove back to Tacoma, watching the early morning light signal the dawn of a new day. I wish that I could say that this was a successful ending but it was not. Georgia and Jerry walked away from the facility because those in charge would not let them stay together since they were not married.

Like birds returning to old nesting places, Georgia and Jerry somehow found their way back to Tacoma. The city was more than a place where they knew how to get drugs. Law enforcement officials were always ready to do their duty. The "two for the road" became again two for life behind bars.

I last saw Georgia and Jerry when they were again separated. Georgia was held in a prison for women not far from Tacoma. When I heard where she was, I visited her. She was glad to see me but very depressed. When she was transported to St. Joseph's Hospital in Tacoma for some special medical treatment I visited her. She was not alone in her hospital room. Two armed prison guards were sitting not far from her bed. This was the last time I saw Georgia.

I saw Jerry when he was held briefly at the state prison on McNeil Island. When I talked with him in the special visitation area I mentioned that maybe prison was a good thing for him because he could not get drugs here. He informed me that drugs were available in prison but did not go into detail. This surprised me given the careful screening I was subjected to before getting on the prison boat.

My last personal encounter with Jerry was when he was a resident in the prison for men at Walla, Walla, Washington. After identifying myself at the reception area I was escorted to an area for visitors. I waited some 45 minutes for Jerry to appear. When he did I could see that he had spent a lot of time on personal grooming before he felt ready to face me. He had no other visitors. I was a "priest." This was a very special time for him.

My last contact with Jerry came in the form of a telephone call. Sometime after my visit at Walla Walla he called me collect from a small town in Mexico. He said that he could not find work. I did not encourage him to return to the States, knowing that this would again place him in the no-win situation of drugs and jail or prison.

I do not know the final scenes in the saga of Georgia and Jerry. I left Tacoma at retirement. My own personal space was shadowed by trauma. I will share some of this when I detail my last 50 mile runs as benefits for my night ministry.

Thin, blond, twenty years old and dancing with drugs:
Mary was a regular on the downtown streets of Tacoma. She was an attractive young woman with a serious problem of addiction. When I saw her on the street she always had a smile for me. But she squirmed and twisted her fingers as she avoided my eyes when talking about drugs. One night, however, she said that she wanted to

take classes to become a beautician. Her dream was to get off the streets.

This young blond was generally with others, making it hard to engage her in serious conversation. One night when she stood alone on the sidewalk she held out her arm for me to see the noticeable inflammation along her needle tracks. She said that she had been in the hospital. The infection episode from excessive injections of drugs scared her. Her arm had swollen up "like a football." She felt that she had to do something. Her solution was to reduce her intake of drugs. She was doing "only" two shots of heroin a day. Based on her normal pattern she felt that this was a sign of progress. But she was still living with a man who was actively dealing drugs.

A few weeks later, Mary came running up to me on the street. She said that she had been looking all over for me. Earlier in the day she had been released from jail after serving a two-week sentence. She was proud of the fact that she had been off drugs for that amount of time. She said that she came down to the street that night just to prove to herself, her friends and me that she could say no. So far she had been able to refuse all offers of drugs. While in jail she attended a church service. She was surprised to learn that God would forgive her. As she saw it, she had done far too many "bad things." The image of this young woman with a sparkle in her eyes and an eagerness to reach out to people haunts me as I realize how deeply she was involved in the drug culture of the city streets at that time.

A 15-year-old runaway:

It was after midnight. I was tired and feeling like I should call it a night. But I decided to make one more round of the downtown streets. As I passed a bus stop area I noticed two fellows sitting back from the sidewalk. One of the two noticed me and called out as I approached. As I moved closer to the two strangers, they appeared as a study in contrasts. One was an elderly man who was wearing a heavy jacket. He was lost in a rhythmic action, moving his arms constantly and staring vacantly into space. It was not possible to include him in a conversation. The other fellow was a young boy. This boy, Jim, said that he was 15 years old. His brown hair fell down over his eyes and covered his ears. He wore tennis shoes with no shoestrings.

Jim wanted me to know that he was a runaway from a group home in the city. He had been on the run for several days, going to Seattle where he ate and slept in a mission. As he saw his situation, one of the other boys in the group home was "out to get him." Fear of this other boy was the motivation for running away. But now he wanted to return. It was getting cold. He did not have a coat. He was hungry. He did not have any money.

I called the runaway hot line and the police and waited with him for an officer to arrive. What does a 15-year-old runaway think about on the downtown streets? Jim wanted to talk about the church services he could remember. Obviously, the presence of a "man of the cloth" served as a reinforcement for such talk. But I wonder if the thoughts would not be present even if they were not so reinforced. As he kicked at the concrete curb with a well-worn tennis shoe, Jim broke into the spontaneous singing of stanzas from gospel songs.

Another significant area of interest for this kid of the streets was memory about his parents. He talked for some time about his father. I was informed that the father played a musical instrument in a local band and lived "not far from here." There was never a negative word about the father. Jim also spoke about a stepmother. Again, there were no words of condemnation. At the time I wondered if these parents knew that their teenager was a runaway and that he really cared about them. When the police officer came and Jim left I was thinking of my own family situation, both in the past and in the present.

"Can you help me do a funeral?"

Ray, a man in his 30' wore a brown shirt and clean blue jeans. His skin was a darker shade of brown than the shirt. Late one night he called me aside on a downtown street. I could not remember meeting him before, but he seemed to know who I was. When we were out of sight from others on the sidewalk, I noticed tears in his eyes. He was holding a tin can with coins in it. Ray's first words to me were; "I don't know how to do a funeral, could you help?" Then he told me that his young wife had died. He was taking up a collection to pay for her cremation. He wanted her ashes to be thrown overboard out in the bay. Ray asked if I would go along in the boat, say something appropriate and then release the ashes. I hesitated for a minute, wondering if this was a set-up to get rid of me. But Ray's sincerity seemed real and so I agreed.

I should not have been so hesitant. As it turned out, Ray was never able to follow through on any of the funeral details. I set up a time to view the body with him. He did not show up. I learned later that he was in the hospital under treatment for both a heart problem and withdrawal from heroin. When he was released from the hospital I talked with him about new plans for a funeral. But when the specific time was set Ray was again not available. This second time he was in jail.

The young woman was buried. Only her parents and a few close family members were present. Ray was very mad at the family for making decisions without him. They, in turn, were very bitter toward him and his lifestyle which they felt had something to do with their daughter's death. I listened to one very angry telephone conversation between Ray and the mother of the deceased. In the course of this conversation, Ray informed her that he had always felt that she was against him in the inter-racial marriage. He went on to tell her that he made more money in one week that she made in a whole year. I assume that Ray was selling drugs and also working as a pimp.

Trying to fly into the cuckoo's nest:

I took a call from Tacoma General Hospital in Tacoma after 1: AM. Emergency Room personnel were concerned about a 27-year-old woman. This woman was not going to be admitted. She had no place to go after hitchhiking from Seattle, headed for the state mental hospital near Tacoma. She really thought that she could simply admit herself into the state hospital. When I met her I could see that Jill was carrying a very heavy load of anxiety. The nurses said that she did have a minor physical problem but that her major issue involved mental illness. Two days before this late-night encounter, she had attempted suicide. Most of the time she was able to work and take care of herself in her own apartment while taking regular medication. But now she was in acute stress. When I saw her she said that she felt like "everything was falling apart," and that "no one was interested" in her.

I knew that someone does not simply walk into a mental health hospital. Normally, a mental health professional becomes involved. This professional initiates the intake process. Jill really wanted to be admitted. In talking to the medical personnel at Tacoma General I learned that Jill was considered a "difficult case" in Seattle, her place of residence. She was inclined to abuse the system, making it hard for professionals to take her seriously when she did get into a crisis situation. She had been in a number of different clinics during the day before I saw her late at night. In one of these clinics she was restrained with leg holds while waiting for an examination.

Ultimately, I was left with the decision about what was to happen to Jill that night. I did not feel that it would be right to dump her on the street at that hour of the night. I encouraged her to return to her home in Seattle, 30 miles away. In doing this I knew that if she agreed I would be the one to give her a ride home since she was without funds. When she agreed with this plan of action I walked her to my car and we started driving north on the freeway. After I was up to my normal highway speed she started talking about jumping out of the car. I slowed down, stopped on the shoulder of the road and let her calm down before resuming our trip.

Jill had a very good memory for addresses and directions. She gave me detailed instructions about how to get to her place. I talked with her about all of her possible options at this time of the night. She said that a hospital 10 miles beyond her home had admitted her in the past. We drove past her normal turnoff, heading for this hospital at her request. It was now 4:30 AM.

In the waiting room of this second hospital only one other person shared the facility at that hour of the evening/morning. This other person was an elderly man who was waiting for word about his wife. She had suffered a heart attack that night. I sat with Jill in the waiting room. When she was paged to report for an exam she insisted that I go with her. I walked with her back to the examination room and waited with her until the physician on duty entered the room. Then I stepped outside, returning after the exam to wait with her for the decision. A call was made to the psychiatrist in residence. They decided to admit Jill. When she picked up her bag to leave the exam area I noticed a large Bible on top of other personal items. I left her with a word of blessing before driving home in the early morning dawn of a new day.

Fear around intimacy:

When connections between people become intimate this can become the basis for fear and anxiety. Fear of AIDS can become a major issue. I sometimes became involved late at night with someone who was primarily concerned about the issue of AIDS. One night, for example, in Tacoma I spent some time talking with Rick, someone I had seen before. We met in an all-night restaurant where we moved to a booth where we would be out of the hearing range from customers at the counter. In this booth there was some small talk and then this man, in his early 30's, told me that he was worried because "they" had told him that he needed to take a test for AIDS. He had no idea why he had been singled out for this test. It was not in connection with employment.

Rick told me that he was very cautious in his sexual behavior. That night he desperately needed someone to talk to. We explored all options, including the possibility that the test would come back positive for AIDS. I primarily offered emotional support when he needed it. Rick thanked me profusely for the dialogue. I did see him on several other occasions after this encounter. He was much relived to get the test results indicating that he did not have AIDS.

For some on the night scene the AIDS fear was a primary driving force. As one part of this scenario, I saw folks who had no real reason to think that they had the disease, but they lived under the cloud of having AIDS. Late one night, for example, the bartender in an affluent cocktail lounge asked me to go over to talk to a man he saw as in "bad shape." I found a man who had been drinking and who was eager to talk. For starters he said that he had been evicted from his apartment and did not know where to go. He also talked about police harassment.

When I seemed like a good listener, this stranger in the night lowered his voice and then said that he would tell me his real problem. At that point he said that he had AIDS. Then he started to cry. He had told no one else about his disease. Then I was given details about the time three years before when he had heard about his test results. After listening to this man and then meeting him on other occasions, I concluded that he did not, in fact, have AIDS. He did have emotional problems. He had adopted the AIDS diagnosis to complement the round of problems he personalized as part of his life style.

"I'm no good to anyone:"

One evening I stepped into the cafeteria section of a late-night place in Tacoma that also had a cocktail lounge area. No one sat at the lunch counter. I ordered a cup of hot chocolate, chatted with the waitress, and then started to walk out the front door. As I walked past a booth, a middle-aged man caught my attention. His body language announced that he was sitting in a pit of deep depression. I stopped and sat opposite him in the booth. When I said "Hi" he simply stared. We sat in silence for several minutes and then again I said "Hi." This time he was able to come up with a weaker version of the same greeting.

This stranger dropped his anonymity to become a real person as he gave me his name, Ben. During a conversation that staggered with lapses when he said nothing, Ben told me that he had not been to work in three days. He had not called his wife. He had been doing some drinking. His words focused mostly on his feelings of total failure. He informed me that he was "no good to anyone." Then Ben said that he had attempted suicide a few years before. He could not think of any reason to keep moving on. He was convinced that his wife would never take him back, and that he would never get his job back.

When Ben said that he was going to simply wander the streets in his state of utter dejection, I suggested that he call his wife. He told me that he could not do this, and that she would not speak to him anyway. At this point I asked for the telephone number. When he gave this to me I went to the pay phone back in the hall leading to the restrooms and dialed the number. When his wife answered and I identified myself she was glad to hear from me. She told me to bring her husband home.

It was then my responsibility to offer Ben a ride home, some six miles away from the night spot where we met. On the drive he said that he just had to stop for a cup of coffee. I purchased a cup for him at an all-night donut shop. Then we continued the drive to his apartment. There was some hesitation on his part when we stopped in front of the building. I walked with him up two flights of stairs. When his wife responded to his knock on the door she thanked me profusely for bringing her husband home. I followed up on Ben, meeting him again by appointment at the apartment. In addition to his wife taking him back, he also got his job back.

"I'm going to kill someone:"

Sometimes I stopped in an inter-racial tavern on old K Street in Tacoma. In this place it was not unusual to see one man displaying a hand full of white powder and another man showing a roll of bills. Violence and drug dealing where the specialties of the house. My presence, wearing the white clergy collar, was something of an enigma in this night spot. The police would sometime drive by and shine their spotlight into this dark place. I wonder what they thought when they caught me in the light.

On one of my visits two men started arguing. Facing each other in an open space, they exchanged threats. Since there had been a shooting only a few days before in this night spot, people sitting near this potential fight immediately leaned back away from the line of fire. After some loud threats and arm gestures the two combatants separated.

As I was leaving one of the two would-be fighters motioned for me to sit down because he wanted to talk. His first question for me was; "where is the nearest Catholic Church?" Then he said that he needed to go to confession because he was going to kill a man. This stranger of the night went on to inform me that he needed someone to help him through his growing feelings of anger and desire to kill. I stayed with him for some time, talking about his thoughts of murder and better ways to handle his situation.

All in a night's work:

On one dark night along the drug strip in downtown Tacoma, I had conversations with several people, all seriously involved with drugs. One man had turned to illegal drugs after using legal pain medications. A woman was addicted to heroin but wanted to get into drug treatment. Another woman needed to talk about her boyfriend who had recently been released from jail.

But the two contacts that have become most vivid in my memory point to both "success" and "failure" when walking with someone heavily into drugs. The success came in a contact with Jim. When I saw him on the street at night this young man never appeared as someone who could command attention on the stage. But before his career in drugs he had been a professional musician. He told me that he never made less than $50,000 a year. His picture was on the front cover of music magazines. Drugs changed all of this. I saw him and his brother in jail and as they wandered the streets in tattered jeans.

But on this night when I saw Jim he first expressed guilt at being found on the street again. He said that he was making progress in getting his life together. One of his problems, as he saw it, was that he felt that I had always been there for him, but that he had not given much in return. In prior conversations he had mentioned that his mother lived just out of town. This night I suggested that maybe he needed to go home and that I would take him. He hesitated briefly, but then agreed to go with me. As we drove south on Pacific Avenue he said that he at least needed one more beer. I told him that he did not need this. At his mother's place we talked about his going into treatment. Jim did follow through. I saw him some weeks later when he was visiting a friend in the hospital. He was looking forward to returning to his music career.

I wish that I could report similar progress for Ray, the man I first introduced around the problem of doing a funeral. This night I saw Ray again. He had been in jail again. As he greeted me this night he reached out a hand in greeting and said that he was "getting it together." But his companions and presence on the drug strip suggested otherwise. A few weeks before this encounter I had gone to visit Ray at his request during his recovery from a brutal knife attack. He told me that he had died "five times" on the way to the hospital and in the hospital. Now he seemed to be recovering in spite of his loss of some lung capacity from the wound. When he said that it was about time for him to talk about his soul I encouraged this. But I told him that he would need to change to see God, he needed to approach God in a different way than he handled other relationships. He was heavily invested in being a con artist. He would need to surrender, to become a different person than he was. His response to this challenge was to put an arm around my shoulder as we walked across a downtown intersection. His total response told me that he was not yet ready for a serious spiritual journey. I never saw Ray again.

"Where's the reverend:"

When I think of Jill I think of a lovely flower hidden in a green bulb, wanting to bloom but unable to. It is hard for me to share my walk with this young African American woman who shouted out the question above in the empty hall of a hospital one night. In sharing this story, I am thinking how far I had come from the time many years before when I drove down country roads to visit people as we shared in the living room of their comfortable homes. Jill alternately slumped to the floor and staggered forward toward an exit in the hospital. Although I was walking beside her, with an arm around her shoulder, assuring her of my presence as I guided her back to the emergency room she would call out "where's the reverend?" At the time Jill was going through withdrawal after a long run of cocaine use.

That night started when I saw her standing alone in the middle of a downtown sidewalk. She was in deep pain. I immediately put an arm around her and told her that I could not stand to see her suffer like this. I said that I would take her to detox and get her started on a treatment program as I walked her to my car.

As we drove through the streets of downtown Tacoma I felt the personal agony of watching a friend writhe in the physical misery of a body out of control. She nodded off to sleep. Then she awoke with a start, arms thrust out. Unaware of where she was. But conscious of my presence.

My first goal was to get her to the emergency room of a local hospital which had a large alcohol/drug treatment program. I knew that I could not take her to the small public detox faculty because at that time they were only open to people going through withdrawal from alcohol. With considerable effort I was able to help Jill struggle into the emergency room of the large hospital. A medical technician on duty informed me that there was no public detox facility anywhere in the city or anyplace in Seattle/King County immediately available at that time of the night. In desperation I asked if the hospital could keep my friend over-night while I worked on a plan for treatment.

After a professional huddle the staff told me that they could offer three days of detox for $1,500. I was not happy. The professional service was completely out of the cost range for Jill and for my program of ministry.

Out in the parking lot as we walked in the darkness toward the car, Jill said simply that she wanted to go home. She thought that she could just walk a block or two, not aware that she was in a different part of town. I said that I was not ready to give up. I wanted to try another hospital. We drove across town and walked into another emergency room. This time I was told that they might be able to admit her if she had some problem in addition to drug withdrawal. Hoping that they would find a broken bone or something else of medical interest, I suggested that they examine her.

It was at this point that Jill wandered off down a long hall, looking for an exit and crying out for me. When I got her back to the E.R. area, with the help of a security guard, she nodded off in a deep sleep. The physician on duty said that she might sleep for as long as six hours. It was now 1:30AM. I asked the staff to watch her and then to call me when she awoke. I made my way home, but found it hard to sleep as I lay in bed, thinking of my friend and the hopelessness of the case. I tossed in bed that night, occasionally drying tears with the bed sheet.

At 6:00 AM I was paged to return to the hospital. Jill was just waking up. I helped her stand and walked her again to my car. My new plan was to get her some breakfast and then to follow the recommended steps to get her into treatment. When I showed her the menu at a fast-food restaurant she pointed to a $3.95 breakfast special and asked if that was too much money. I said that she should order what she wanted. Although she had not eaten in three days she only poked at her food, putting most of it in a doggy bag to take along when we left the restaurant.

Over breakfast Jill talked about her feelings when she saw women working as waitresses. She said that she was overcome with a sense of envy. She added that she really wanted to have a regular job. We talked about a vocational training school and the kind of work she might be able to get into. She also told me that she really wanted to get her son back and that most of all she wanted to be free of drugs.

After breakfast I drove to the local office of the Department of Social and Health Services (DSHS). This office opened at 8:00AM. We were the first two people to enter the building when the doors opened. This was a necessary visit because it was the first step in getting financial support for treatment through a fairly new program, the state's Alcohol and Drug Addiction Treatment and Support Act (ADATSA). With approval from DSHS the interview process could begin at ADATSA in another building across town.

I walked up to the intake window at DSHS with Jill. She was given a stack of forms to complete. She tried her best to stay awake for this chore but kept nodding off. I took over the task, asking her questions, completing the forms and telling her where to sign. This was a difficult task, but we did complete the work. I assumed that she was now on the way to treatment. But this proved to be a very naïve assessment of the situation. At the intake interview window, the person on duty looked at the forms and complained that some of the boxes were not filled in. The corrections were made. Then we were told that the system was over-taxed and that we would need to come back in a week for the actual interview. At this point I knew that I had lost the battle. A person actively addicted to cocaine was told to go back out on the street to encounter regular offers for drugs while waiting for an intake interview!

I was left with few options. I drove Jill back downtown and cried as I said goodbye to her. She did have an appointment card for an interview which was set for one week into the distant future. That seemed like an eternity away at the time. I drove back to DSHS on the day of the interview but she did not show up. Several nights later I again saw her on the street at night. She was strung out on drugs, very agitated, striking out at buildings and people and expressing deep feelings of guilt about her failure to keep the appointment at DSHS. I also saw her getting out of a car late at night in another part of town which made me anxious that she might be turning tricks to buy her drugs.

One might wonder how I could develop such strong feelings for this person of the night. There were times when she would run across a downtown street to greet me with a hug and a kiss on the cheek. I was present when she was very depressed and ashamed of her appearance. I also saw her when she was very neat in appearance. She often greeted me with words like "Rev. Dean" or "Father" and "it's so good to see you." During my times of contact, she asked me to visit her father in the hospital. He had major circulatory problems which necessitated the amputation of one leg. I called on him in the hospital. The other leg was also amputated. I then visited him in his home when he was released from the hospital. These and many other contacts pulled me into a pattern of sincere caring and concern for Jill. I really wanted her to walk tall through life. But I lost contact with her. She remains as one of many truly important people who now live only in memory for me.

Native American tragedy:

Harlan, a 29-year-old Native American, had stringy, black hair that fell freely from under his faded ball cap. His face was covered with different colored spots of skin. He was not a handsome young man. But after meeting him in a tavern that catered to Native Americans, I developed a strong sense of wanting to be part of his life. We would pull away from the bar to find a booth where we could talk. It was unusual for me to be in this night place. People in another tavern a few blocks away on Puyallup Avenue warned me that the place was not safe. It was true that violence of one kind or another was not unusual around the place. But there were also people like Harlan and they were the focus of my ministry.

When I learned that a relative of Harlan's over in Montana had died I gathered some funds so he could make the trip to attend the memorial. Harlan was an alcoholic. While he was in Montana he tried to jump a wire fence and broke his leg. He returned to town with heavy bandages on this leg. A few weeks later he was picked up by the police at night and charged with a misdemeanor. I visited him in jail. He was going through withdrawal at the time. I did not see him in a regular visiting room but did see him through the window of his cell. He was scooping water out of the toilet and throwing it on the wall.

When Harlan was released from jail early one morning I saw him on the back stoop of the tavern. His crutches did not follow him out of the jail. I talked with him as he struggled to take a standing position. I hugged him and told him that I was going to do something to get him into treatment for alcoholism. On the Friday before Christmas of that year I went out to the tavern where we met to tell him that I had managed to raise some money so he could get into treatment over near his tribal land in Montana. When I opened the door of the tavern I was met by several of his friends. They told me that Harlan had died. From gangrene! He was sleeping outside and did not change his bandages. I cried and vowed to get out of this work. It was just too painful. Nobody should die at the age of 29 from gangrene! But I stayed with the work for another 8 years.

Karen was another Native American tragedy. She was a princess. Her father was the chief of one of the tribes in Western Washington. Before his death he was an outspoken advocate for Indian rights. Karen had an income from her legacy in Indian lands. But she was also heavily addicted to drugs. I saw her in jail, in her apartment when friends were visiting and on the street at night. I talked with her about her addiction and did the best I could to get her into some kind of treatment. Then one night I heard that she had died from an over-dose of drugs in the women's restroom of a cocktail lounge on Puyallup Avenue.

On The Run Again

At night other people set the pace and determined my direction. When I set out to run in the morning I set the pace and I determined my direction. In Tacoma we lived in a small house near the University of Puget Sound. I could run to several destinations before turning around for the run back home. Sometimes I ran down to the boardwalk along the shore of Puget Sound. Other times I ran to one of the near-by parks.

I have always been drawn to Mount Rainier, the majestic mountain with its snow covered high hat, just south of Seattle. As I have shared, I came to Tacoma with a reasonable amount of experience in long distance running. While struggling with some way to finance the work of Operation Nightwatch- Tacoma I considered a benefit run from near the entrance of Mount Rainier National Park into Tacoma. I drove out from lower Pacific Avenue in downtown Tacoma on State Highway 7, past Mineral Lake to the small town of Elbe where I took State Road 706 to near the Park entrance, for a distance of 50 miles, to survey the route I would run, taking pledges for each mile completed. As it turned out, I ran this distance three times, each time a benefit for my work at night. The town of Elbe was familiar to me since I had given a sermon in the historic Elbe Evangelical Lutheran Church on one occasion.

Stella was my back-up support for the first two of these 50 milers. She took me out to the starting point in the early morning and then followed me along the road back to town. I carried water and Gatorade with me on the run. On the last of these 50 mile runs a friend, Alan MacArthur drove out to the starting point with his young daughter and then got out of his car at different points to give me some added support.

The Fifty Milers

It's Never Just Running

These words are an easy cliché. Of course it is never just running. I finished two of the 50 milers with Stella as my support team. When I ran into a finish area in Tacoma after the second run I was not too exhausted to ask her to go home and get my dog, Duchess. I stood in the park with my dog to accept the congratulations of friends. At the time I assumed that Stella would walk with me into the sunset as we spent the rest of our life together. We had been married for 45 years at this point.

One fateful day a few months after my second major run into Tacoma I received a call from Stella. She was at her office in a Presbyterian Church where she planned events for seniors. She asked me to join her at the church. I drove across town for the meeting. She said that we would talk in a room down in the basement of the church. I followed her down the stairs. After we were seated for a few minutes a woman I had never seen before joined us. Stella introduced her with the words: "This is my attorney and she has the divorce papers." I was totally caught off guard. I had no idea that she was planning this. I cried and said that I would sign anything. The attorney ended the meeting by praying. I did not appreciate the attempts to sanctify this sad time by holding the meeting in a church and by the prayer. I drove home in tears.

Stella had arranged to stay with a woman friend until after the divorce was final. I never saw her in our "home" again. I was allowed to stay in the house for two months and then had to leave since the house was her property, according to the divorce. The bathroom floor needed to be replaced so I did that, knowing that it would be hard for her to do. I also purchased a bathroom shower unit, planning to install a new bathroom area on the second floor. I did get up on a tall ladder with a chain saw, intent on cutting a large space to allow for the intrusion of the bathroom unit. But at the time I was still recovering from a fall in a roller-blade accident during which I broke my right arm in three places. I could not manage the saw, so I gave the project up. My task was to hunt out my personal belongings from the attic and the garage so I could make a clean exit from what was at one-time communal property. I left some flowers and the house keys on the kitchen table before leaving the house to begin I knew not what.

Lots of my fingerprints and memories will always remain locked in that house in Tacoma. I installed a gutter system up on the roof. I painted the entire exterior. Unfortunately, the house did not have an adequate heating system. At the time wood burning stoves were popular. A small stove had been placed in one corner of the living room. It was not an adequate heating system for the house. An old oil furnace was buried in the crawl space under the house. I cut an opening in a downstairs bedroom and managed to pull this relic out. Then I installed a drain system for the crawl space and hired a team to install a new heating system. Out in the yard I monitored a garden space and maintained the lawn and a border of flowers.

Maintaining a house is not the same as maintaining a marriage. I knew that the relationship had grown cold but never, ever imagined divorce. My work at night did not help. A couch with pull-out bed claimed a large space in one downstairs bedroom. When I came home from my late shift on the downtown streets I simply made up this bed so that I did not bother her in the large bed for two upstairs. I was not out late every night, only two or three nights a week. Sometimes I slept downstairs even when I had not gone out for my work at night. There was a TV in my downstairs sleeping space. Most nights I watched TV while she spent the time reading a book in the front room.

What do you do when you are suddenly single at the age of 63? I attended a divorce recovery group at a local church. We were told that we should not date anyone in the group. But I saw an attractive woman, near my own age, and started dating her. This became a serious affair. It was good for her but I had the growing feeling that I wanted out of the relationship.

Walking, Not Running, On A High Bridge

These words deserve their own byline. They share a very important event in this account of my life journey. After the divorce and after becoming involved in a relationship that I wanted to end I was in San Diego, talking with some pastors about starting a night ministry for that city. One morning I went for a long walk. I was very depressed but did not talk to anyone about my plight. This is interesting because my brother Darold, also a minister, and his family lived in San Diego. On my long walk I came to a high bridge. For the first time in my life I was thinking about ending it all by jumping from the bridge. A woman was coming from the other side in the walkway across the bridge. I considered asking her to walk with me across the bridge but changed my mind and walked off by myself.

Life has brought me many blessings since that day. I will share some in the pages of this book that follow. One immediate blessing that remains with me is the number of people who respond when I share this story with words to the effect that they are glad that I did not jump. This always gives me a good feeling. Given my personal experience and my walk with others when they were suicidal I know that it is very important to engage others in conversation. Unfortunately, even within extended families the talk about important things is sometimes most noticeable by its absence.

A Companion for My Third and Last 50 Miler:

I did run the 50-mile distance from near Mt. Rainier National Park into downtown Tacoma three times. As I have shared, Stella, my first wife, was my support team for two of these runs. When I decided to run the distance a third time I was 65. More importantly, I was dating Joan, a woman who owned a dry cleaner in Tacoma with her husband. I was a regular customer and always enjoyed seeing Joan as I left or picked up dry cleaning. I never dreamed that I would have the privilege of becoming her husband. One day when I went to the Cleaners Joan was not around. I asked her husband where she was and was told that she was down in California with one of their sons and that they were separated. Then he did a strange thing. He gave me her address in California. I think that he assumed that I would try to encourage her to return to him. I did write to her. I did not see her in California but we wrote to each other. When she returned to Washington she was separated from her husband of 37 years and filing for divorce. She moved into her own apartment in Seattle. We started seeing each other after her divorce. She was my support team for the third major run. I completed that 50 miler at the age of 65 in 8 hours and 35 minutes. This event was covered by the Tacoma News Tribune with the headline; "65 is not the limit."

Joan was devoted to the Roman Catholic Church. She had been a member all of her life. It was very important for her to be married in her church. I regularly attended meetings of a group for instruction in the Catholic Church; Roman Catholic Instruction for Adults (RCIA) for nine months to become a member of the church of Rome. It was very exciting when I was able to take communion for the first time with Joan. I also went through the mandatory process of annulment from my first wife. Joan and I were married in a Catholic Church with a large number of people attending. This included her four children, Phillip and John from California, Brian from Florida and Teri who lived in Seattle. We had lots of contact with Teri.

Joan made a large down payment on a house in West Seattle. This was on a hill looking out over Seattle. She then paid to have the lower level of this house converted into an apartment that she rented out. Needing a new source of employment, Joan found a job as a cashier for a large Drug store in West Seattle. Wanting a better job, she decided to complete a course of study to become a pharmacy technician. One of the requirements of this course was that everyone was asked to recall a list of some 100 medications and their use. When Joan became sick after a grand mall seizure she was given the option of withdrawing from the course. But she elected to stay and did graduate with the class.

This should have been a secure situation for both of us for years. We were in love. A story waiting for a happy ending. But this was not to be. The first signal that something could go wrong came after a visit to my daughter and her family in Colorado during the winter. We went up to Estes Park to stay in a cabin. It was not adequately heated. Joan developed a cold. When we returned to Seattle she was showing signs of not feeling well. I drove her to a clinic in West Seattle. In this clinic she had a grand mall seizure. She was taken by ambulance to a downtown Seattle hospital. I stayed with her during most of her stay in this hospital. I stretched out beside her in the hospital bed. We looked out at downtown Seattle. We laughed.

Soon after we were married for only one year I again took Joan into a medical facility where she was examined and we were told that she had ovarian cancer and that it was at stage 3 or 4. I did not know what this meant. She went on to surgery and then chemo and radiation. One of her requests was that we say the Lord's Prayer together as she was taking the chemo treatment. She lost all of her hair. I purchased a hat for her and we both went to select a wig. At no time did I think that Joan would die. She was on chemo when I decided to take on two more marathons, one in the tri-city area of central Washington and the other up in Vancouver, Canada. I took her with me to both of these marathons where she waited patiently for me to cross the finish line. I was 67 at the time. Of course I have deep regrets. I never asked her what she wanted to do with the idea that she needed something like a "bucket list". That was never on my mind since I was in total denial in terms of the possibility that she would die.

After a few months Joan was placed on the hospice list. This meant that we had a volunteer come to the house. He offered to do whatever was needed, shopping, etc. At around the time of what would have been our 2nd wedding anniversary Joan was admitted into a residential hospice facility. I spent a lot of time with her in this hospice place. I was with her all night the night before she died, after being in the facility for only three days. I was holding her hand when she died at 9AM.After only two years of marriage I sat through a memorial service for her in the same Catholic Church where we were married only a short time before.

Looking back at this dark time for me I really wish that someone from the medical community or someone from the church had been more straight-forward with me. We had a visit at the house from the woman who would do the homily at her memorial service that was only one month away. This woman spent her time talking about the politics of the church. At no time did she allow a word about death or dying to escape from her lips. The staff of the hospice facility was kind and did a good job. But again I only wish that they had been more straight forward about the nearness of death.

One good spot for me in all of this is that I started attending a bereavement class which was sponsored by the hospital that took care of her originally. It was helpful to listen to others and to share my own feelings in this group. The leader was very encouraging about people in the group going about the business of re-building their life. I remain thankful to Joan for all that she was and for her true love of me. I am also very thankful that I have been able to go on with life. If you are one who has gone through major loss I can reaffirm the truth that talking about it helps. I am feeling much better now that I have typed out the words to describe the death of Joan. I was very apprehensive when I began this part of the book.

With the death of Joan and given my age it was time for me to leave the Seattle-Tacoma area, time for me to start the new walk into retirement. I will share some of the more recent events in my life in the next and final chapter of this book. The Tacoma program was unable to continue when I left the area.

Chapter 7

Running and Living After 70

As I write this before committing it to my computer hard drive I am aware that I am now 83. In the process of considering the sights, smells, sounds and dreams of my life I am tempted to think of myself now as an old car. Is an old man like an old car? The car has been over the road. It has lots of miles, has been to lots of different places. It has some dents and the finish shows signs of ageing. Time to curl up in a warm garage. Time to stop crawling up mountain roads.

In reality, an old car is a poor metaphor for an old man. A car is one-dimensional. It can move along a road, but little else. An old man can see, feel, dream. This morning as I was on a bus on South Boulder Road, headed for the campus of the University of Colorado in Boulder I was keenly aware of the sights and sounds around me. I marveled again at the sight of the Flatirons, barren, rock hillsides standing at erect attention to guard the entrance to the majestic, snowcapped Rocky Mountains.

On campus I audit classes. This semester I am escorted back in time to consider the men, women and children caught up in the tragedy of the Holocaust, genocide or mass murder as I sit with students cradling new lap tops in an anthropology class on the Holocaust. Lectures and films surround me with the horror of mass murder in Turkey, the Ukraine, Germany and Poland as well as along the shores of a sandy creek not far from the shadows of the city of Denver back in the mid-19th century.

Another class gives me a free ride up into the stratosphere as I ponder objects and distances in a class in Introductory Astronomy. It is very, very hard for me to imagine distances measured in light years. Or to comprehend the kind of heat and physical forces at work constantly at the core and pushing toward the surface of the sun at all times.

Prior to sitting in classes my routine includes walking over to the University Memorial Center where I find a table for my mid-morning tea. From my back pack I retrieve a small thermos bottle and a fresh donut in a plastic bag.

Words are powerful. But they never come close to capturing the essence of life, of relationships, dreams and all that goes into a day for an old man or a young man. An old man is not "like" an old car. There are memories of the past, experiences today and dreams of the future. Unfortunately, our society is saturated with views of the young or middle-aged. Voices of the "elderly" are too often muted.

Dean Jones at 83 years old

In this chapter I share my journey from the age of 70 to my present age of 83. It will be the last of my memoir writing. But I do expect to be out jogging well after I turn 84.

To Berkeley, California

When I was 70 I found myself headed south on Interstate 5 in Washington State, driving from Seattle in my Toyota Camry, headed for Berkeley, California with my cat, Myrtle. Looking back, I find it interesting that my last venture away from Seattle traced part of the route I took 53 years earlier when I ran from home. This time the trip was uneventful. The Berkeley destination came after a friend helped me get a Visiting Scholar position at the Graduate Theological Union (GTU). I would spend a year on the campus, across the street from the University of California at Berkeley. This would give me the opportunity to audit classes at will.

My first challenge in Berkeley was to find a suitable apartment, one that would accept a cat. I did locate a studio apartment, not far from campus renting for $840 a month. This gave me one room which served as living room and bedroom plus a small kitchen and a bathroom. I purchased a few items of used furniture and set up housekeeping. GTU is an ecumenical campus, with several different seminaries sharing the same turf, both Roman Catholic and Protestant. Some of the seminarians were returning to college life as part of a mid-career change of course. They were not all freshly out of college. I did not feel out of place at my age of 70. Of course I was much more than an older man sitting at a desk. I carried with me the shadows of both a surprise divorce after 45 years of marriage and the equally surprising death of my second wife after only two years of marriage. The Berkeley experience was a time of recovery for me.

Introduction to Thomas Merton:

"Nobody started it; nobody is going to stop it. It will talk as long as it wants, this rain. As long as it talks I am going to listen."[4]

The few words above come from the book "When the Trees Say Nothing" by Thomas Merton. Looking back at the experience, I am surprised that it took me so long to become acquainted with the works of Thomas Merton. My favorite class at GTU was one taught by a Jesuit priest titled "Contemplation and Action." In this class I was transported back to the life and world of the renowned Trappist Monk. Merton reached beyond creative writing to write with true inspiration. He could weave a new tapestry around the sights and sounds of birds and flowers surrounding his hermitage. A routine assignment of walking through the monastery at night as part of the security patrol became again an experience infused with images giving a profound sense of something far from the ordinary. On a visit to Louisville, Kentucky he stood at the corner of 4th and Walnut and the sight of everyday people was for him a transforming experience. Unfortunately, Thomas Merton did not have the opportunity to write in his 80's. He never saw his 60th birthday, dying an accidental death at the age of 53 when he was on a special trip away from the monastery in Bangkok, Thailand in 1968.

In addition to attending classes with seminarians, I also shared in other ways. I attended daily chapel services. These were always inspiring. I also took my lunch to campus and ate with the students. On occasion I walked across the street to wander around the campus of the University of California at Berkeley.

Dirt / noise and an old sleeping bag:

I soon returned to my old habit of running every morning. On my first run down University to the Marina I met an older man who wore dirty blue jeans and walked with some effort. This man, Howard, had made a temporary camp up under the bridge carrying cars into downtown San Francisco. The floor of his bedroom was dirt. The noise from cars passing overhead was a constant throughout the night as he tried to sleep in his old sleeping bag. He was old but not old enough to draw social security. He had some health problems that made it difficult for him to become a regular part of the work force.

Every morning I arranged green lettuce, slices of fresh lunch meat, yellow cheese and mayonnaise between two slices of white bread for my lunch. This sandwich, together with some fruit and cookies was nestled in a small, brown paper bag to accompany me up the hill to the campus. But I also made a second lunch and put it in another bag together with a dollar bill which I carried with me on my morning run to give to Howard. I am sure that he appreciated my daily ritual of sharing lunch with him. Several months into this routine he simply disappeared. After a few days I saw him again on the sidewalk near his old "home". His first words were… "The police came and took me to jail...then they trashed all of my stuff." This made him become more creative in securing a sleeping space. He informed me that he was sleeping somewhere "secret" where the police could not find him. I made arrangements with him to drop his lunch at a designated place. I continued this lunch drop and he always managed to pick it up. I never saw him again and did not know where his new space was.

Dating after 70:

70-year-old male. PhD in sociology. Taking ballroom dance classes. Avid long distance runner. Now living in Berkeley, California.

The words above appeared on an internet dating site together with contact information as I continued to explore the new land of being single. On campus I did notice a few women not too much younger than me who seemed like possible "dates." But nothing serious developed. I did journey off campus to attend dance classes at a large ballroom not too far from campus. Since I had never danced in my younger years this was all new to me.

I did find a few women through the internet dating service. My major problem with this experience was that I did not post a picture of myself on the web site and responded to some women without seeing their picture. In one case a woman flew out to California from somewhere back east to meet me. When I saw her at the airport I immediately knew that she was not someone I could be serious about. I did have the opportunity to meet a number of women through the internet. I always thought that it would have been much better to simply meet someone during the course of the day and then approach them about a date. But times have changed. Old neighborhoods no longer exist. People are on the move. The internet seems to be creeping into every part of our life.

I have good memories of my year in Berkeley. But I knew that I would be moving to Colorado where I could be close to my daughter, Kathy, her husband Ken and their two children, my grandchildren, Nathan and Ryan. My son, Steve, and his partner, Sonny, lived in the Seattle area. Before moving to a more permanent apartment in Boulder County I decided to spend the summer in Leadville training for the Leadville 100. I was now 71.

The Leadville 100 Mile Run

Leadville, Colorado would not be selected as an ideal place to run. Nestled in the range of the Colorado Rocky Mountains, this town claims an altitude of 10, 152 feet. This is not a recommended altitude for running. But the Leadville 100 did not require a qualifying 50 miler so I was anxious to test myself. So I spent the summer running on trails used in the 100 miler and looking forward to race day.

I did not take the time to explore the town during my three months of residence. Leadville has a very interesting history. Some days I ran along the Mineral Belt Trail up above town. This trail took me near the site of the Matchless Mine. In the silver mining days this was one of the sites claimed by Horace Tabor. He and August Meyer founded Leadville in 1877. With the rush to claim and develop local silver mines Leadville became the second largest city in the country with a population of 40,000 in 1880. By 2010 only 2,602 people claimed Leadville as their home. In its high day it claimed visitors with the renown of Oscar Wilde and Doc Holliday.

My wife Ruth and I recently went on a tour that included the restored cabin on the site of the Matchless Mine which was last used by Tabor's second wife, Baby Doe. Although Tabor made a fortune in the business of silver mining he lost this fortune to become nearly a pauper at the time of his death as the standard for coinage in the country changed from silver to gold. Before his death he told Baby Doe to stay with the Matchless Mine. He honestly felt that another wave of silver riches would come. Baby Doe lived on the site, alone. She walked into downtown Leadville for supplies. One winter after she had not been seen in several days someone went to the cabin and found her frozen body. There was firewood in the cabin. She most likely died of natural causes and then the body froze.

When I stayed in Leadville for the summer I was not in town for a historic journey. I was intent on running. Every day I ran from my apartment in town out a road and up to Turquoise Lake. I often ran around the north shore of the lake to the May Queen Campground and then back home. The organizers of the 100 mile run also planned a 26 mile run from May Queen to Twin Lakes. I ran this part of the route for the full 26 miles. As the trail drops down into Twin Lakes it becomes narrow as it winds along a cliff. This was not a welcome way to end the 26 mile run.

One night during this summer experience I was not feeling just right. My first thought was that I was having a problem because of the less than normal oxygen flow given the altitude. I drove myself to the local ER where a technician checked my blood oxygen level. He then informed me that my count was better than his! So I drove back to my apartment and had a good night's sleep. I was surprised a few days later when a doctor at the hospital called to see if I was O.K.

I was told that the 100-mile race had been organized as a way to bring in tourists. I knew that I would have 30 hours to finish the course. All runners would be timed at Aid Stations. If a runner was not up to the speed determined sufficient to finish the race this runner would be asked to leave the course. On the day of the race I gathered in the dark at 5 AM with the other runners on Main Street, not far from the historic Tabor Grand Hotel. I was one of only three runners who were over 70. As it turned out, none of us in this geriatric set was able to complete the full 100 miles. When the gun went off to start the race I began running with a flashlight in my right hand. We would run down city streets and then out a road leading to Turquoise Lake. I had run this route before in training. Near the lake it was necessary to climb up a rocky slope. On this slope I saw a woman who was staggering like a drunk. At first I thought that perhaps she did not have a light in the darkness. But that was not her problem. She had entered the race after coming to Colorado from near sea level. She was suffering from the high altitude. I was not able to do much for her, only encouraging her to keep going until she came to the next Aid Station.

I ran as a new day dawned. At the first check point at the May Queen camping area I was cleared to continue. I knew that some runners were coming up behind me. I crossed a road and continued up a hill on a road used by vehicles in the maintenance of utility lines reaching across the hills. Then I came out on a real road on my way to the Fish Hatchery. Near this spot an official stopped me to tell me that I was not up to the expected speed. So my wrist band was cut and this ended my only 100-mile attempt. This was also my last official long distance event. When I was 79 I did jog up and down Lookout Mountain for the last time.

What can I say about my failure in Leadville? This book, of course, is about more than running. The primary focus has been on direct involvement with people in a number of serious situations. As I have shared, I walked with men and women in the shadow land of homelessness, alcoholism, drug addiction and suicide. You may be reading this as someone who is actively involved in a helping profession or you may be preparing for such a career. One take home lesson is that we do not always succeed. I did not succeed in Leadville and I did not "succeed" in some of the situations where I became involved late at night. You cannot always count on success, either in running or in trying to help people. On the other hand, my Leadville running experience remains a very memorable experience for me. I ran down streets and on trails against the back-drop of high, snow topped mountains. Every day I was captured by the lovely sight of Turquoise Lake. In failure there was a kind of "success." All of those I touched at night remain as part of my memory trail. I can honestly say that I am thankful for the opportunity to know them, in and out of jail, in the sharing of their dreams, in being part of their life journey.

Move to Boulder, Colorado

After my Leadville summer I moved to Boulder County so that I could be close to my daughter, Kathy, her husband, Ken and their two children, my grandchildren. I was then able to become involved in many activities with Nathan and Ryan, not realizing at the time that the window for doing this would not be open for too many years as they naturally grew into young adults with a life of their own.

I spent some time at a special grandparent's camp with both boys up in the mountains. This gave me the rare opportunity to share a cabin with each boy individually and to take part in the activity of the camp. One night I was watching a movie with Ryan in a building down the hill from our cabin. He fell asleep during the movie and I carried him up the hill to our cabin. I also climbed with him up into a special area, a "hidden room" in the rock formation out of camp.

With both boys I recall very special moments with them when in a cabin their parents had for a few years out of Fairplay, Colorado. One night in this cabin Nathan came down where I was sleeping on the lower level very early in the morning. He sat beside me as together we watched the sun come up for a new day. A few months later I took him to see the Harlem Globetrotters when they were in Denver. Now, as I write this, Nathan will be starting his final year as an undergraduate with a major in pre-med and Ryan is looking at his last year in High School.

Finding Love in a Ballroom Dance Class

I continued to date, using an internet dating service. I also met women at places like a county western dance place near downtown Denver. It was during this time that I enrolled in a ballroom dance class in Boulder. Ruth was in this class. She was the most attractive single woman in the class and ten years younger than me. Ruth was a licensed Real Estate broker and office manager for the largest Real Estate company in Boulder. We started dating and were married a few months later. The wedding attracted a good crowd of family and friends. The ceremony was held at a special wedding facility where we were able to offer all of our guests a special dinner. I am blessed to again experience love at this time in my life.

One attraction is that we have both always been involved in the Church. Ruth was a member of a local Episcopal Church, St. Mary Magdalene. Now we are both members and attend regularly. Another mutual interest is the inspiration to be lifted from the high mountains which wait just west of Boulder. Driving up to Rocky Mountain National Park and taking a short walk along the road somewhere is a must.

Ruth and I have been able to take some trips and would like to do more. We joined others for two ocean cruises with Holland America Lines. One took us up the Inland Passage to Alaska. We marveled at Glacier Bay and the sights in small towns along the way. We also took a cruise from San Diego to special sites in Mexico including Cabo San Lucas. The Alaskan cruise gave us the opportunity to visit some of my family in Washington State. In San Diego we spent some time with my relatives who live in that city. On another occasion we went to Pittsburg to visit Ruth's son, Tom and his wife Cheryl.

For me, one of the advantages of this third marriage is that I have been given the opportunity to spend some time with two more children, Ruth's granddaughters, Grace and Laura. They are the children of her son Kurt and his wife, Julie who also live in the area. Grace, now 13 is very talented in playing the flute. Laura, now 10, enjoys sports including running and many other things. Both are now finding a new role in the care and management of a new dog, Rosie.

Ruth has always been attracted to Golden Retriever dogs. Eight years ago she adopted Cinnamon, a large Golden from Golden Retriever Rescue of the Rockies (GRRR). Now 10 years old, Cinnamon has proven to be very good in every way. Ruth took her to classes to be a therapy dog and now takes her to a hospital to give comfort to patients and staff. A few months ago Ruth adopted another dog from GRRR, a small dog with fur of light brown and white, she is a very pretty dog. Only some two years old, Lily is a good companion for Cinnamon. They seem to have adopted each other. Both remain inside all day long. They play together and do a lot of sleeping. At night both dogs join us in our bedroom where they have their own beds on the floor.

Ruth is very attentive to my needs. She is a good cook and prepares a balanced meal every night. As I have mentioned, she sends me off to classes at the University of Colorado in Boulder with a good lunch and snacks for tea time.

I have a large extended family and truly love everyone in this circle. I look forward to any opportunities to visit with them. I will write another book to be titled; "Sermons from a Small Town" and I want to take on another running challenge when I turn 90.

Dean C. Jones

Endnotes

[1]Taylor, Barbara Brown. *Learning to Walk in the Dark*, Harper Collins, New York, 2014.

[2]Jones, Dean C. *The Other Chamber: A Portrait of the Mentally Ill Offender*, Self-Published. Tacoma, Washington, 1996

[3]Jones, Dean C. *Walking Where the Sails Met the Rails: A Venture into Tacoma's Past*, Self-Published. Tacoma, Washington, 1989.

[4]Merton, Thomas. *When the Trees Say Nothing*, Notre Dame, Indiana, Sorin Books. 2003, p.143.

www.ingramcontent.com/pod-product-compliance
Lightning Source LLC
Chambersburg PA
CBHW052148110526
44591CB00012B/1898